Bc

GENESIS and the Christian LIFE

DAILY DEVOTIONS AND BIBLE STUDIES

A Division of G/L Publications
Glendale, California, U.S.A.

THE KING'S INSTITUTE
THE CHURCH ON THE WAY

Quotations from:

Living New Testament, Paraphrased (Wheaton: Tyndale House, Publishers, 1967). Used by permission.

Living Lessons of Life and Love, paraphrased by Kenneth N. Taylor (Wheaton: Tyndale House, Publishers, 1968). Used by permission.

Living Psalms and Proverbs, paraphrased by Kenneth N. Taylor (Wheaton: Tyndale House, Publishers, 1967). Used by permission.

The New Testament in Modern English, copyright J. B. Phillips, 1958. Used by permission of the Macmillan Company.

Today's English Version of the New Testament. Copyright © American Bible Society 1966. Used by permission.

Four Prophets. J. B. Phillips. Copyright by The Macmillan Co., 1963. Used by permission.

Living Prophecies, paraphrased by Kenneth N. Taylor (Wheaton: Tyndale House, Publishers, 1965). Used by permission.

The Twentieth Century New Testament. Published by Moody Press, Chicago. Used by permission.

Published by
Regal Book Division, G/L Publications
Glendale, California 91209, U.S.A.

Library of Congress Catalog Card No. 73-112034
ISBNO-8307-0046-3

CONTENTS

A teaching and discussion guide for use with this book is available from your church supplier.

Chapter 1

START WITH GOD

If you were writing a book that covers the whole history of mankind, how would you begin?

The Bible starts with God. "In the beginning God created." That is the most important truth of the creation story. Everything begins with God!

Here with unmistakable clarity is the doctrine that God is eternal and God created the universe. He laid the foundations of the world. The universe is not an accident, not the result of some capricious uniting of atoms. The universe is the result of God's creative act according to His plan, made for His glory. How firm a foundation for our faith in Him and in His plan for our lives!

Bible reading for this week: Genesis 1:1-4.

1

1st Day   Our Wonderful Lord
Colossians 1:11–20

It is easy to become so involved with the details of the creation story that we forget the Creator. What happened when is not nearly as important as who did what.

Paul wanted the Colossians to put the emphasis where it belonged. The Scripture passage begins with Paul's prayer for the people. Read again verses 11–14.

Then he comes to the heart of the matter: who the Lord Jesus Christ is and what He has done. It seems that Paul cannot find enough superlatives to describe the Lord. Verse 15: "Christ is the exact likeness of the unseen God. He existed before God made anything at all." Verse 16: "Christ Himself is the Creator who made everything in heaven and earth, the things we can see and the things we can't." Verse 17: "It is His power that holds everything together." Verse 18: "He is the Head of the . . . . church . . . He is first in everything." Verse 19: "God wanted all of Himself to be in His Son." Verse 20: "Christ's death on the cross has made peace with God for all by His blood" (*Living New Testament*).

Now, just look at that list again. We worship a wonderful Lord! When you realize that He is such a great God—powerful, infinite, eternal—and yet He loves us. He created this earth and then came down to live on it as a man and to give His life for our salvation. When we think of these things, the details of how the universe was created do not seem so important. We are willing to say with the writer of the book of Hebrews: "By faith—by believing God—we know that the world and the stars—in fact, all things—were made at God's command; and that they were made from nothing!" (Hebrews 11:3, *LNT*).

For further consideration, read the Scripture passage in Colossians from one of the newer translations. Continue on to the end of the chapter. List what you learn about Christ from this passage. What difference do these truths make in your daily life?

2nd Day   Do You Want the Light?
John 1:9–13

Have you ever tried to find your way through a dense fog? Or walked along a trail at night without a flashlight? Even the familiar is not recognized and you soon get a sort of desperate feeling. You have lost your ability to relate one object to another or yourself to your surroundings.

The Lord knows that if we were left to try to fathom Him or walk in accordance with His will we would fail. So, John tells us in our Scripture that the Lord has provided what we need. There is "the light [that] shineth in darkness" (John 1:5). We start with God and we have the privilege of walking in His way guided by the Lord Jesus Himself, the true Light.

It is important to note that the Bible does not speak of Jesus Christ as *One* of the lights. He is called *the* true Light. Truth is not relative despite what we are sometimes told. Often the reasoning goes like this: The Ten Commandments are *sometimes* not applicable. Everything depends on the situation. This is the "new ethics." Under this system there are no evildoers, enemies or wicked persons.

The idea may be called new, but it is as old as

mankind. The reasoning began with Adam and Eve and has been practiced by every generation since that time.

In John we read that Jesus Christ, the true Light, was rejected. He came to His world, but it did not want to know Him. Even His own people did not receive Him. And the people remained in darkness.

God did not create sin. He created man with the freedom of choice. If man did not have this freedom he would be a beast or a robot. But man is free to choose—stumble in darkness, or walk in the Light. That's the only alternative.

For further consideration, read all of the prologue of John's Gospel, John 1:1-18. Note the names or descriptions that are given to Christ. What do you think each one tells us about His personality or His work? What does each mean to us in our relationship to God?

3rd Day   The Hand of God   Job 12:7-15

One of Job's friends, Zophar, had just called him stupid. (See Job 11:12.) In our Scripture reading Job is answering the accusation. He has been brought low, Job admits this. See verse 4. But Job adds, "Look around you. Look at the creation of God. Consider the animals, the birds, the earth, the fish. Everything tells you that God's hand is upon them all. Then, it is only logical to understand that the hand of God works in the lives of men."

Those words of Job read easily—if you are comfortably seated in a bright and airy room, the temperature just right, nothing particularly bothering you. But suppose you were in Job's position. You have lost all your livelihood and hope of earning a living, your children have been killed in a natural catastrophe, and you are covered with boils. Can you see the hand of God at work in your life now? Job could.

He goes on in verse 11 and says, "Just as my mouth can taste good food, so my mind tastes truth when I hear it" (*Living Lessons*). Considering Job's circumstances, this too is a statement of great trust in God.

In verse 13 he summarizes his ideas. "True wisdom and power are God's. He alone knows what we should do; He understands" (*Living Lessons*). That is good to acknowledge and even better to live by. He made us and He knows us and He understands us. Now, what should our response be?

There is a great responsibility in living. Your life is a gift from God to be lived to His glory. What a terrible thing to accept the gift and ignore the giver and throw the gift away. What a privilege to accept the gift and seek to glorify God who gives you life!

For further consideration, check a Bible concordance for the words "breath" and "breathe." What can you learn about glorifying God from some of these verses?

List the things you learn about God in the Scripture passage from Job. What do you think is Job's main idea in answering his friends this way?

4th Day   Can You See?   Psalm 19:1-6

To many, God is the *great unreality*. Some reject Him or the idea of Him, because to think about the existence of God appears to them to be incomprehensible. Others give Him no thought at all. Still others are afraid of Him and so they try to ignore Him.

It is not possible to be neutral on the subject of the existence of God. Anything less than a definite affirmation of belief in Him is a denial. Even a plea of ignorance is inexcusable.

God has seen fit to reveal Himself in the Scriptures. He shows that He is powerful but gentle. Compare Psalm 19:1 with Psalm 103:13. He is beyond finding out, yet He leaves traces of Himself everywhere. Compare Isaiah 55:8, 9 with Psalm 19:1. With mighty strokes He hews out valleys, fills rivers and oceans. He creates; He reveals; He sustains. And He makes demands of His creatures.

Why is God so unreal to some people? Apparently one reason is that they do not really want to be convinced. Longfellow spoke of the problem in *Aurora Leigh:* "Earth's crammed with heaven, And every common bush afire with God; But only he who sees takes off his shoes—The rest sit round and pluck blackberries."

All heaven is crammed with God, too. But only those who look for Him see Him. The Russian cosmonaut couldn't find God in space. But another group of space travelers read Genesis 1. It is all in the way you look at God's creation.

This may be what David meant when he said that the heavens declare God's glory. Look again at the Scripture passage in Psalm 19. There is no place in the universe where the reality of God is not proclaimed by His creation! In Romans 1:20, the apostle Paul says that anyone who looks at God's creation and denies His existence is without excuse.

6

For further consideration: What are ways you can come to know God's power without being afraid of Him?

What can you learn of God by looking at the universe He has created?

Why is God so unreal to many people? Is He unreal to you?

5th Day   Man Enters the Picture
Genesis 1:26-31

The work of creation was almost finished. The Lord had made the heavens and the earth. The earth was made beautiful and was populated with animal life. The heavenly lights had been placed in the sky. All was ready for the crowning act—the creation of man. And with the coming of man came the statement, "let him have dominion" over the rest of creation.

Here was a new dimension added: a steward acting in behalf of his master. "The earth is the LORD's," the psalmist wrote (Psalm 24:1). He was right. The earth is the Lord's and man was put here to act as a steward over God's creation.

How did the steward do? The Bible, history, and our own experience answer that question with embarrassing directness. The steward failed.

Environment is not the answer. Adam and Eve failed in the perfect environment of the Garden of Eden.

Heredity is not the answer. The descendants of Noah failed, and they came from the line of a man who "found grace in the eyes of the LORD" (Genesis 6:8).

Technology is not the answer. The people failed

on the plains of Shinar as they built a great tower toward the heavens (Genesis 11).

The wisest man who ever lived found that his wisdom was not the answer. He concluded "In much wisdom is much grief: and he that increaseth knowledge increaseth sorrow" (Ecclesiastes 1:18).

There is no doubt about it—as a steward, man is a failure. How gracious of God not to let us remain in our failure. Man started as a steward, and became a slave. (See Genesis 3:17–19.) Then through the sacrifice of Christ, those who believe in Christ are elevated to sons and John says that is not the end of the story. He says, "See how very much our heavenly Father loves us, for He allows us to be called His children—think of it—and we really *are!* . . . Yes, dear friends, we are already God's children, right now, and we can't even imagine what it is going to be like later on. But we know this, that when He comes we will be like Him, as a result of seeing Him as He really is (I John 3:1,2, *LNT*).

For further consideration: What does it mean to you to be called a child of God?

Read Jesus' parables about stewardship. See Matthew 18:23–34 and 21:33–40. What do these teach about the duties of a good steward?

6th Day   Worship the Creator   Psalm 24

This is a worship psalm. It was read as the people came to the house of God to praise Him. If you look at the psalm carefully you will see that there are two reasons given for the service of worship.

First, because the world belongs to the Lord. He

created it—founded and established—the psalm says. The earth belongs to God, the earth and everything that is in it. In light of this ownership, we who live in the earth should worship God.

Second, we should worship the Lord because of who He is. This thought is implied throughout the psalm. There is the preparation for this worship. Since God is God, those who come to Him should be sure they have been prepared to meet Him. Clean hands, a pure heart, honesty and truthfulness are required characteristics of the worshipers.

Then there is the preparation which we receive from God. He gives righteousness as a gift, for He is the God of our salvation. He makes our hands clean, our hearts pure. He empowers us to be honest and truthful. It is only reasonable that we seek Him and we worship Him. He is God and He gives good things to those who seek His face.

Finally the psalmist says we should welcome the Lord. And He will come to us. What a privilege! What an amazing thought! When we come to worship God, He comes to us. The God of creation, the Lord of our salvation, the King of glory, comes to us!

For further consideration: We often think of the Lord as our friend. When we know Jesus Christ as our Saviour, He is our friend. But now, spend a few minutes considering the greatness of the glory of God. Take a Bible concordance and look up the word "glory." Find the times that the Bible speaks of God's glory. Jot down on a separate piece of paper what you learn about God's glory. Think about what you write. What difference should the truths make in your worship of your Lord?

How great is your God? In this psalm David seems to be overwhelmed with the greatness of his God. Are you ever overwhelmed with God? In *Living Psalms and Proverbs* the first verse reads like this: "I bless the Lord: O Lord my God, how great You are! You are robed with honor and with majesty and light! You stretched out the starry curtain of the heavens." Then further on in verse 5 we read: "You bound the world together so that it would never fall apart." Further on again in verses 7–9: "You spoke, and at the sound of Your shout the water collected into its vast ocean beds, and mountains rose and valleys sank to the levels You decreed. And then You set a boundary for the seas, so that they would never again cover the earth." It just seems that the psalmist cannot find the words he needs to tell all of the greatness of God.

We who know the Lord Jesus Christ as our Saviour and so know God as our Father often lose sight of the greatness of God. To us He is the friend who sticks closer than a brother. To us He is the one who is always available to hear us when we pray and to satisfy our every need. Now, there is no doubt He is all these things, but He is also the great God described by David in this Psalm.

It is good for us to pause every so often and contemplate what a great God we love. It is worth recalling that the Lord we love and serve is the Lord of creation, the maker of heaven and earth. He is our friend when we have received His Son into our lives. But let us never forget that He is also our God and He should be revered and honored and we should stand in awe at His greatness and His majesty.

10

In verse 29 we read: "If you turn away . . . then all is lost." Let's never forget how much we need to depend on God.

For further consideration, read all of Psalm 104. If possible read it also in one of the newer translations. Notice how the psalmist covers the Creation in his description of God. Notice especially the conclusion that is reached in the last verse. Do you reach the same conclusion?

Stop for a minute and think about God's creation. Remember when you have stood before some natural wonder—a waterfall, a tall mountain, a vast canyon— didn't you feel small and insignificant? God made that by speaking a word! Tonight look up into the sky. It seems so far away—those stars look so little. You are seeing only a small part of the universe. God made it all by the word of His power. David, the psalmist, felt like you. He said, "When I look up into the night skies and see the work of Your fingers—the moon and the stars You have made—I cannot understand how You can bother with mere puny man!" (Psalm 8:3,4, *Living Psalms and Proverbs.*)

But God does bother with "puny man." In fact, He loves you no matter who you are. How do you think you should respond to such a great God who loves you so much?

Chapter 2

CREATION: "BEHOLD, IT WAS VERY GOOD"

The Bible says that God looked at the things that He had made and found them to be very good (Genesis 1:31). You and I look at the creative works of God and we stand in awe of the One who has such power and wisdom.

Our response is nothing to be ashamed of. The writer of Proverbs says that "The fear of the LORD is the beginning of knowledge" (1:7). To fear God means to stand in awe of Him. The word carries with it the idea of being cautious lest He be offended, to stand in reverence because we realize who God is.

We worship a great and wonderful God, so let's continue to fear Him and to worship Him and to serve Him with our whole strength.

Bible reading for this week: Genesis 1:31—2:9.

1st Day   The Last Word   Hebrews 1:1-4

Throughout the Bible there are numerous passages which describe creation in a variety of ways. This week we will be reading a series of them. The first is today's verses taken from the Epistle to the Hebrews.

Here is the sustaining power of the Lord Jesus Christ, God the Son. Read again verse 3. Notice that the passage begins by pointing out that the Lord Jesus is unique. God gave many revelations of Himself and His plan throughout the Old Testament. But the final revelation is the Son. And it is almost as though the writer added "And thus endeth the speaking."

Then follows a list of descriptive statements regarding the Son. Verse 2: God gives all things to His Son. The Son is the agent of creation: "by whom also he made the worlds." Verse 3: The Son shines with the glory of God. Is God. Upholds or sustains all things. All of these describing the Son and His work in and with creation.

Then the writer of Hebrews moves on to a different phase. He has described the eternal Son of God. Now He tells us of the Son who became a man for our sakes. "He is the one who died to cleanse us and clear our record of all sin" (LNT).

Then the emphasis moves back to the glory of the Son of God who is seated in honor at the right hand of the throne of God.

What a wonderful God we have. He has made the world, revealed Himself and His plan. Then He has made provision for us when we do not live up to His commands. He has sent His Son, whom He loves, to earth for us that we might have forgiveness and cleansing from our sins.

13

The God who creates is powerful and we stand in awe of His glory and holiness. The God who saves is merciful and we bow in gratitude for His mercy and forgiveness.

For further consideration, read the whole first chapter of Hebrews. Make a comparison chart between the Son and the angels. Add a third column for what might be said in the same vein about you as a Christian. For example: Christ is God's Son. Angels are God's messengers. As a Christian I am a child of God. One of the newer translations may help you.

2nd Day   None Can Compare
Isaiah 40:12–14

Isaiah gives another description of the Creator. In Hebrews we read of the sustaining power of the Son of God. Now Isaiah describes the Creator's power and wisdom.

Consider the way Isaiah chooses to impress us with the greatness of God. The prophet looks first to the oceans. God, he says, cups them in the palm of His hand as you would hold a few drops of water.

Then, he looks up to the heavens. God measures these with a span, Isaiah says. A span is the distance between the tip of the little finger and the tip of the thumb when the hand is fully extended. God measures the heavens by spreading His hand across them, Isaiah says.

The prophet isn't finished yet. He gives us the picture of the Creator carrying the earth in the type of basket that people used to measure produce. God puts the mountains in the scale, the pan used for weighing, Isaiah says.

Nations are like a drop in the bucket. He picks up islands as though they were a speck of dust. All the forests of Lebanon, the cedars you know, couldn't make enough fuel for an altar fire. There aren't enough animals to make a sacrifice.

That takes care of the power and might of the Creator as far as Isaiah is concerned in this instance. Now, what of His wisdom? Read verses 13 and 14. He needs no one to advise Him or even talk things over with Him.

The conclusion is self-evident. But just in case there is a question Isaiah states it in verse 18. God is beyond compare! No one can be likened to him!

All of this is a little frightening. Such a great God. Where do we fit in? Read the verse that precedes our passage—verse 11. Does that answer your question? Such a great God and yet He cares for His own as tenderly as any shepherd watches over his sheep!

For further consideration, read Psalm 139. We have made a list of the greatness and majesty of God from Isaiah. Now make a list from this psalm of what God is and does for you. Thank Him for His love and concern!

3rd Day   An Examination   Job 38:1–11

By the time Job heard the words of our Scripture passage, he had been saturated with words and arguments. The story of Job and his loss of property, family and health is well known.

In his plight, friends came to visit him. The first, Eliphaz, told Job that he was quick to talk to others and encourage them when they were in trouble, but Job could not handle the problem when trouble came to him. (See Job 4:1–5.) Job answers that he wishes God would let him die (6:8,9).

The second speaker was Bildad. He told Job that his problem was the result of sin. If Job were upright he would not have trouble. (See 8:1–6.) Job's answer is that all are sinners, so why should he be the recipient of so much trouble (9:1)?

Zophar accuses Job of self-righteousness. (See 11:1–6.) Job denies the accusation and says that he has as much understanding and is as good as any of them (12:1–4).

Finally Elihu spoke. He was angry at Job for trying to justify himself (32:2). Elihu spoke of God and the power of the Lord. To him Job had no answer.

God spoke next. In our Scripture passage are the opening verses of this discourse. Did you notice that much of what God says is in the form of questions? It is God asking Job about many things, and Job unable to pass the examination. In the beginning God spoke of creation. "Where were you when I laid the foundations of the earth?" God asks. Can Job explain about the stars? Or, can he explain the workings of the ocean and the tides? Job is silent: "I lay mine hand upon my mouth," Job says (40:4).

God continues to speak. At last Job is made to realize that he is not perfect before God. He needs forgiveness from the God of creation. And at last Job repented (42:6).

We have been reading of God's work of creation. It is about time to do some soul-searching. How do you feel before the God of creation? What will you do as a result of what you have read?

For further consideration, read the additional Scriptures mentioned above. Apply the experiences of Job to yourself. How do you stand? Spend time in prayer considering whether there is any change necessary in your attitude toward God.

4th Day   Wait upon the Lord
Isaiah 40:27–31.

Do you ever get discouraged? Then, this Scripture portion was written for you. Several days ago we read a portion of Isaiah 40. The great and powerful God, the Creator of all things was presented in majesty and He was declared to be the only God.

Now the prophet Isaiah moves on to another truth about the Creator. Just to keep our point of reference clear, Isaiah reminds us that he is talking about the everlasting God, the Creator of all things. He further repeats the truth that no one can comprehend Him—He is beyond us in wisdom and understanding.

But having reiterated these points Isaiah speaks his words of comfort. The mighty God gives strength to His children. One translation of verse 27 reads like this: "O Jacob, O Israel, how can you say that the Lord doesn't see your troubles and isn't being fair?" (*Living Psalms*).

Isaiah lived in the days of the Assyrian conquest and eventual capture of the Kingdom of Israel. In light of the wars, the sieges, the hardships which the people of Israel were enduring they became more and more discouraged. The Israelites were no different from us.

17

They began to blame God and doubt His concern for them. It is to this attitude that Isaiah speaks.

God has not forgotten Israel. And God does not forget you when you are His child. Even the young men may give up, but those who wait upon the Lord will find their strength renewed, not dissipated. In exciting times of seeing God at work, "they shall mount up with wings as eagles." But in the everyday grind of the usual, when circumstances seem so normal it gets tiresome, "they shall walk, and not faint."

Discouraged? Then wait upon the Lord. That is, exercise patience in His steadfastness, faith in His concern, and assurance in the knowledge that He will supply whatever strength you need.

For further consideration, remember our hindsight is so often better than our foresight. Take a piece of paper and, thinking back over the last several weeks, list the times that you can see God worked in your behalf. Thank Him for it! Thank Him for working in times you are not even aware of yet!

5th Day   Praise the Lord   Psalm 33:1–9

Today we come to another of the Scriptures which instruct us in our response to the Creator. We have read who He is and we have read of His greatness. We have been told that He cares about us and our needs. Now, this psalm says, "Praise the Lord."

That is good advice but we need a little more help. For what shall we praise Him? The psalmist gives us a list. Verse 4 says, "The word of the Lord is right." This word "right" is the same as that used in Isaiah when he speaks of making the crooked paths straight.

In other words, God's Word is not devious. Praise the Lord for this.

In the same verse: "All his works are done in truth." The word "truth" carries with it the idea of steadfastness or faithfulness or trustworthiness. We might say that we can depend upon God and what He does. So, praise Him!

Verse 5 tells us that God loves righteousness. And also we read of the goodness of the Lord. How wonderful to have these truths consecutive. That God loves righteousness is a fearful thought, for we are not righteous. But that we may be the recipients of His goodness and His love is a comforting idea. So, we can praise Him!

Next the psalmist tells of the power of God. He made the heavens with a word. He made and controls the seas and puts them where He pleases. When we realize the work of the Creator we stand in awe of Him. But we can still praise Him as we worship Him.

What is the result of the work of God and our response in praise? Read the closing verses of this psalm, 18–22.

For further consideration, read several other Psalms of praise, such as 34, 103, 136, 139, 148 and 150. Meditate upon them. What can you add to these from your own experience? Praise the Lord!

6th Day   God's Provision   Psalm 65:9–13

The goodness and provision of God the Creator is again the theme of our Scripture portion. David spent the greatest portion of his life in the southern sections of the land of Israel. In this area water is in great demand. During the short winter the rains provide a relatively large supply of water. But little of it sinks into the soil. Most flows useless into the sea. Thus the canals and the springs were of great importance to the people of David's day and also to people in Israel today.

David's reference to the river of God in verse 9 may be a reference to the water canals which the people used, and upon which they depended for irrigation during the dry seasons.

In verse 10 the psalmist says that God provides the moisture and then also causes the grain to grow. Thus God's gifts are the means as well as the end result.

The use of water to stress the gift and provision of God is found often in Scripture. Jesus Christ is the giver of living water (John 7:37). The Lord calls the thirsty to come to Him and drink without payment (Isaiah 55:1). Give a cup of cold water in the name of Christ, the Lord admonishes His disciples (Mark 9:41). And from the throne of God flows a pure river of the water of life (Revelation 22:1).

God, the Creator of all, is also the provider of all that we need. What a wonderful God we worship.

Water is of great importance to an agricultural people living near a desert place. What other reasons can you think of that make water a good choice for picturing God's provision for our needs?

7th Day   The Earth Is the Lord's
Psalm 24:1–6

All week we have been reading of God and His work of creation. It seems fitting that we close the

20

week with the affirmation: "The earth is the LORD'S, and the fulness thereof; the world, and they that dwell therein" (Psalm 24:1).

That verse, if we really believe it, settles a number of our questions. From where did the universe come? Who holds the final answer? Does man owe anything to his Creator? It's all there in that verse. God is the source. God is the final answer. You and I are His creatures living here on His earth because He graciously gives us life.

"This is my Father's world," we sing. We are right. In Psalm 50:10-12 the psalmist reports God's words: "For every beast of the forest is mine, and the cattle upon a thousand hills. I know all the fowls of the mountains: and the wild beasts of the field are mine. . . . The world is mine, and the fulness thereof."

Paul, speaking to the Athenians on Mars Hill said, "God that made the world and all things therein, seeing that he is Lord of heaven and earth, dwelleth not in temples made with hands; Neither is worshiped with men's hands, as though he needed any thing, seeing he giveth to all life, and breath, and all things" (Acts 17:24,25).

It is all true—this God whom we worship needs nothing from us. But He is so gracious that He will accept from us our prayer and praise. Listen: "What I want from you," God says, "is your true thanks; I want your promises fulfilled. *I want you to trust Me in your times of trouble, so I can rescue you, and you can give Me glory!*" (Psalm 50:14,15, *Living Psalms*).

Will you give Him what He asks?

For further consideration, read all of Psalm 50. This is a personal dialog between God and His people. We no longer bring sacrifices to a temple, but much of what the Lord says about form of worship is applicable today. Consider how He might address the members of your church. What would He be apt to say to you?

A few days ago we read some of God's words to Job. Job 42:1-6 records Job's response to God's words. *"Then Job replied to God:* 'I know that You can do anything and that no one can stop You. You ask who it is who has so foolishly denied Your providence. It is I. I was talking about things I knew nothing about and did not understand, things far too wonderful for me. (You said,) "Listen and I will speak! Let Me put the question to you! See if you can answer them!" ' " The verses which we read from Job 38 were some of those questions. They continued on through chapter 41. Read the whole passage.

Job goes on: " '(But now I say,) "I had heard about You before, but now I have seen you" ' " (*Living Lessons*).

You have been hearing about God all week. Have you by any chance seen Him as well? Job's reaction was to call upon the Lord for mercy and to reject all his questioning of God. What is your reaction?

Chapter 3

MADE FOR A PURPOSE

The worlds were created. The earth was bearing fruit. Animals, birds, fish were all in their places. Everything was finished—except God's final creative work. Everything was ready and so God made Adam.

He created the worlds by speaking them into existence. But when the Bible describes the creation of man we read, "And the Lord God formed man of the dust of the ground, and breathed into his nostrils the breath of life; and man became a living soul" (Genesis 2:7).

Bible reading for this week: Genesis 1:26—2:4.

The creation of man was different from that of any other creature. Man is unique in the plan of God. How does he fit into that plan?

1st Day Look at Yourself! Psalm 8

For two weeks we have read of the greatness of God and the vastness of His universe. Now, when we take a look at ourselves we seem mighty insignificant.

We have seen pictures of our earth taken from the comparatively short distance of the moon. As seen from the vastness of space we must live on a tiny spot of a globe! Then, think of all nations of the world. Ours is just one of so many. And we are just two people in that nation. A number on a census report. What can one person mean when we think of all of God's creation?

David felt like us. He looked up into the night sky and saw just a little of what God had made and he could not understand why God knew or cared about him.

But David went on in this contemplation. He noted that God had made him just a little lower than the angels. God had given him glory and honor. He had rule or dominion over the works and creatures God had made. You can take a look at yourself, and through the Lord Jesus Christ you can say the same things about yourself that David said. God thinks highly of you.

When you realize the truth of this Eighth Psalm, you will want to say with David, "O Lord our Lord, how excellent is thy name in all the world." You just won't be able to praise and thank Him enough.

In the background Scripture in Genesis 1 and again in Psalm 8 we read of man being given dominion over the earth. Look up the word in a dictionary. What do you think man's responsibility is with regard to God's giving him dominion over God's works of creation?

2nd Day   The Value of a Man
Matthew 12:9–13

What is a man worth? Chemically, not much—less than $5.00. Judas sold Christ for a little more than $30.00. In today's evaluation, it will depend on whether the question is answered before or after taxes. What are you worth? That's hard to say.

In the Scripture passage we read today, the people of Capernaum seemed to feel that a man was not as important as the keeping of the letter of the law. He was not as important as a sheep who was in danger of being destroyed.

What value did God put on man? That's a different picture. In the passage we read, Jesus Christ, God's Son, broke the narrow confines of the Sabbath interpretation and healed a man with a withered hand. Notice that He did not break the Law of God. He did no work to heal the man and neither did the man himself do anything illegal when he held out his arm.

God put still greater value upon man than this act of healing. The Lord God made man in His own image. But He did still more. Jesus Christ came to earth, became a man and suffered and died that men might be forgiven. As a result those who receive Jesus Christ as their Saviour become the children of God.

What are you worth? To yourself, not much. To the contemporary world, very little. To God, you are worth everything. Your worth is beyond comprehension. You may be a member of the family of God.

What are people worth to you? It's something to think about. And thinking about it may change your whole outlook on what you will do with the time God allows you here on earth.

For further consideration, read all of Matthew 12. Notice the number of times the Lord demonstrated that the individual was important. Look for answers to the following questions: Who were these people? Did the crowds agree with the Lord's evaluation of their worth? How did the Lord cut across prejudices?

From the example of Christ what do you learn about your own activities? How can you turn your knowledge into action?

3rd Day   "Life, and Breath, and All Things"
Acts 17:24-28

The apostle Paul had arrived in Athens, the city whose patron goddess was Athena, the goddess of wisdom. The acropolis, high place, was a granite hill rising above the crowded marketplace. Here were temples to several of the gods, but the most imposing building was the fabulous Parthenon built by Pericles in honor of Athena. A huge statue of the goddess dominated the building.

Just to the west of the acropolis is another hill about half as high. This was called Mars Hill. The Greeks believed that the god Mars was tried for murder here on this hill. The twelve great gods of the Greeks acquitted him. As a result the hill received the god's name and it became a place of hearings and arguments. Scholars met here daily just to discuss and argue about any new idea. (See Acts 17:21.)

The apostle Paul came to this hill. In front of him rose the high place and its pagan temples. Just to his left was the center of activity, the marketplace. Paul looked around and then preached the sermon that is our Scripture passage for today. He gave the Athenians a "new idea." He told them of the God who made them; who is the creator of all things. The Greeks believed they were especially blessed by the gods as a superior race. Paul said that God "made of one blood all nations of men."

The Athenians listened and then dismissed Paul. The ideas were too new and they had to think about the apostle's words.

The words aren't new to you. But do you give them any more heed than the Athenians did? Read verse 32.

For further consideration, read all of Paul's sermon, Acts 17:22–31. What do you think he was trying to make the Athenians understand? How many of the ideas that Paul preached in this sermon do you think are important today?

4th Day   "In the Likeness of Men"
Philippians 2:5–11

The Bible is filled with incidents of God's power working in the affairs of men. These are often exciting episodes at which we stand in wonder. None is more amazing than the coming of the second person of the

Godhead into our finite world. The eternal Son of God became a man bound by time and space. The omniscient one admitted there were some things He did not know (Matthew 24:36). The one who was omnipresent was limited to being in one place at a time. When you really think about it, the coming of the Son of God to earth is beyond comprehension.

What do you suppose it was like in heaven when God the Son left that place and was born in Bethlehem? How strange it must have seemed when the second person of the Godhead was not there to receive the praises of the angels but was instead receiving the insults of the people He had created!

In the *Living New Testament* translation of I Peter 1:10–12, we read: "This salvation was something the prophets did not fully understand. Though they wrote about it, they had many questions as to what it all could mean. They wondered what the Spirit of Christ within them was talking about, for he told them to write down the events which, since then, have happened to Christ: His suffering, and His great glory afterwards. And they wondered when and to whom all this would happen. They were finally told that these things would not occur during their lifetime, but long years later, during yours. And now at last this good news has been plainly announced to all of us. It was preached to us in the power of the same heaven-sent Holy Spirit who spoke to them; and it is all so strange and wonderful that even the angels in heaven would give a great deal to know more about it."

Prophets wondered; angels wondered; and you and I find it hard to understand how and why the Lord Jesus should do so much for us. But He has done it.

He made us, and when we receive Him as our Saviour He remakes us. Sin spoiled the image of God, but when we know Christ as our Saviour we are "conformed to the image of his Son" (Romans 8:29).

The concluding verses of our Scripture passage describe the exaltation of Jesus Christ by God His Father. For further consideration, use a concordance and check "the name" of Jesus. How many things can you find that may be or shall be done in the name of Jesus? How wonderful for us that we not only know God is our Creator, but that we also know Jesus Christ as our Saviour!

5th Day   Identified with Us   Hebrews 2:5-9

This Scripture passage is a companion to the one we read yesterday. Both of them tell of the coming of the Son of God to this earth, and of His subsequent glorification by His Father.

In Philippians we read in detail what His coming entailed. Today we read a general statement of real significance. Do you recall that a few days ago we read Psalm 8? In that psalm David spoke of looking into the heavens and seeing the work of God's creation. Then, he went on to say that in light of such a great creation he could not understand why God bothered with him. As you read the verses in Hebrews you probably recognized some of the verses quoted from Psalm 8. But did you also notice that this time they are applied to Christ? The Son of God came to earth and identified Himself with the people of His creation.

The psalm said that man was made a little lower than the angels. Hebrews notes that "for a little while he [Jesus] was made lower than the angels" (verse 9, *Today's English Version*). Christ humbled Himself in this way so that He might suffer and die for our salvation.

The psalm further said that man was to be set over creation. The writer of Hebrews adds "But we do not see man ruling over all things now. But we do see Jesus! . . . We see him crowned with glory and honor now because of the death he suffered" (verses 8,9, *TEV*).

"His holy fingers made the bough
Which grew the thorns that crowned His brow;
The nails that pierced His hands, were mined
In secret places He designed.
He made the forest wherein there sprung
The tree on which His body hung.
He died upon a cross of wood
Yet made the hill on which it stood.
The spear which spilled His precious blood
Was tempered in the fires of God.
The glory in which He now appears
Was His from everlasting years.
But a new glory crowns His brow
And every knee to Him shall bow."°

For further consideration, read the account of the death of Christ in one or more of the Gospels—Matthew 27; Mark 15; Luke 23; John 19. When you compare these accounts with the Genesis account of creation, does it make you realize the tremendous price Christ paid for your redemption? What do you want to do to show your gratitude to Him?

°Source unknown.

6th Day   God's Blessings to Man
Psalm 103:1-5

In light of what we have been reading during the past several days, aren't you inclined to agree with the psalmist as he writes the words of our Scripture reading?

When we think of all that the Lord has done for us we cannot help but be grateful to Him and want to praise Him.

David seems to be reminding himself of all that he wants to thank God for. First, he reminds himself not to forget the gifts of God. *Living Psalms* translates it "the glorious things He does for me." What do you have to praise God for? What are some of the glorious things He does for you each day? Follow David's example and think about them and then praise and thank God for these gifts.

Next, David says that the Lord forgives his sins. Now, certainly we can be even more appreciative for this act of God. We know the Lord Jesus Christ and we know what He did for us to forgive us and cleanse us from all unrighteousness.

At the end of the fourth verse there is another of God's gifts to His children. "He surrounds me with lovingkindness and tender mercies!" Imagine our being privileged to live in the aura of God's love and mercy. Our environment is his love.

Verse 5 says: "He fills my life with good things!" Another translation uses the word, "satisfies." Some of us are hard to please, but if we give God a chance He will satisfy us.

Look back over these few verses and pay special attention to the verbs David uses to describe God working in his life. The Lord heals, redeems, surrounds and satisfies. That's quite a list, and all from just three verses of one psalm. We have a great God to love and serve!

For further consideration, read the entire psalm and continue to list the verbs which David uses to describe the work of God in his life. If possible, read the psalm in more than one translation so that you can get a clearer picture of all that David is saying. Meditate on your list and then thank God for His blessings to you.

7th Day   Bless the Lord!   Psalm 103:15–22

Today we turn to the concluding verses of the psalm we read yesterday. In this section David distinguishes between the brevity of our lives and the everlasting steadfast love of God. We can rely on the Lord. Someone has said, "God is too wise to make a mistake and too loving to be unkind." Of this we may be sure.

As a result of all that David has considered concerning the gifts of God, he ends the psalm as he started it—with a call to "bless the Lord." He calls for angels to bless Him, for His armies and servants to bless Him, for all of creation to bless the Lord. Then, he ends with a declaration of his own determination: "Bless the Lord, O my soul."

What does it mean to bless the Lord? The Jews have written at great lengths concerning how the rules in the Bible are to be interpreted and obeyed. In connection with this determination of David to bless the Lord and to bless His holy name, much has been written. Boiled down, the words were interpreted as meaning that a person should conduct himself in such a way that people would want to emulate him and would want to serve his God.

To bless the Lord would then mean to praise Him, to worship Him, to honor Him and then also to live in such a way that people will be drawn to Him.

That's a big order! Can we do it? With the Lord's help we can! Shall we?

Psalm 104 is another psalm of blessing to the Lord. For further consideration, read it and note that His work of creation is also detailed. How does David describe creation as compared with Moses' description in Genesis 1? Read carefully the last three verses. How will David praise God? What do you think you should do to praise Him?

The first question of the Westminster Shorter Catechism is: "What is the chief end of man?" The answer: "To glorify God and to enjoy Him forever." All week we have been reading passages from Scripture which accept these thoughts. We were created in the image of God, placed upon the earth and given dominion over it. By obedience we would have glorified the Lord. In our disobedience we fail to honor Him.

When we know the Lord as our Saviour and walk with Him as our friend, we cannot help but enjoy Him and our fellowship with Him. We are secure in His love and assured of His power to enable us to do as we should.

We fail; He remains faithful. We disobey; He offers the means for forgiveness. We try to walk alone; He offers His companionship. Read I John 1:6,7.

What is your main purpose in life? Will you glorify God and enjoy Him today and forever? Then tell Him so, and do it!

Chapter 4

ONE MISTAKE

Can you imagine what the Garden of Eden must have been like? I'm sure no matter how hard we try, the picture is beyond our description. A garden made by God especially for His creation. Everything perfect. Adam and Eve made for each other. Their meeting with God every day to have fellowship with Him. No problems, no worries. Just one commandment—"Of the tree of the knowledge of good and evil, thou shalt not eat of it: for in the day that thou eatest thereof thou shalt surely die" (Genesis 2:17).

Life couldn't be better and, in many ways it couldn't be easier!

There was just one question. God had made man with a free will. How would he use it?

Bible reading for this week: Genesis 3:1–15

1st Day   Without Excuse!   Romans 1:18-23

The Scripture readings for this week take us to the book of Romans. We have set forth for us Paul's declarations concerning the condition of man without God's salvation. Sin came into the world through the single act of disobedience in the Garden of Eden. Now as you read the passages from Romans, notice how that one act has grown.

Paul details for us several disturbing statements regarding man's sinfulness. In verse 18 we read that the wrath of God is revealed against sin. This word used for wrath is in itself terrifying. It carries with it the meaning of deep and abiding anger. This is not the quick outburst of displeasure but the settled, abiding condition often associated with revenge.

In verses 19 and 20 we read that the Lord reveals His existence and His power in the visible things of creation. Anyone who does not see God in His handiwork is without excuse. This time Paul chooses to use a judicial term. He speaks of defending one's self before a tribunal. In this instance the individual who will not recognize God's handiwork and so acknowledge His existence is without a defense.

Finally in verses 21-23, Paul says that the people who knew enough to worship God turned instead to the worship of idols they had made. Sin was really bearing fruit. From disobedience, to denial of God's existence, to the worship of other gods, this was the downward trend that man followed.

The picture is not a pretty one, but then sin is not pretty and life without God is less than worthless.

For further consideration, read the rest of Romans 1, verses 24-32. What else does God say about the sinfulness of man? Notice especially verses 28–32. There are a series of descriptive words and phrases. Do you think man without God is really this bad? Does the sinful nature of man seem more graphic to you as a result of this reading? How does this description differ from the common idea of man improving himself?

2nd Day   Before You Condemn, Look in a Mirror
Romans 2:1–5

When we read the list of gross sins in Romans 1, it is easy to fall prey to a sense of superiority. "We never do *those* things" we say as we straighten our invisible halo. Paul has led us along so carefully that we have not realized we have been caught in a trap. Just as we get comfortable in our respectability, he springs the trap.

Paul has just said that the man who cannot see God in His creation is without excuse before Him. Now, to the self-righteous man he says, "Therefore *thou* art *inexcusable,* O man, whosoever thou art that judgest." And he used the same Greek word to describe both men. Suddenly the spotlight of God's righteousness is turned on us, whoever we are.

It is not easy to sit and read the words of this Scripture passage with ourselves in mind. Somehow it is always more comfortable to read about the impersonal "they." But God's commands are personal and we are forced to realize it. Listen now and repent and come to God for forgiveness. Wait and receive the judgment Paul has been describing.

Living New Testament makes this clear in its translation of verses 4–6: "Don't you realize how patient He is being with you? Or don't you care? Can't you see that He has been waiting all this time without punishing you, to give you time to turn from your sin? His kindness is meant to lead you to repentance. But no, you won't listen; and so you are saving up terrible punishment for yourselves because of your stubbornness in refusing to turn from your sin; for there is going to come a day of wrath when God will be the last Judge of all the world. He will give each one whatever his deeds deserve."

For further consideration, read the story of the rich young ruler in Mark 10:17–22. How does his story relate to the passage in Romans? Reread the story of the young man. What is his attitude toward Jesus? What is the Lord's attitude toward him? Where did the young man go wrong? What is the lesson for you?

3rd Day   No Escape!   Romans 2:12–16

In this Scripture passage the apostle Paul takes up another excuse people try to give for their refusal of God's offer of salvation in Christ. In Romans 1 we read that some people deny that God exists and hope to get by that way. But they are without excuse before God. No defense possible!

Then, yesterday we read that there are those who consider they are not as bad as some. Besides, they rationalize they have escaped so far, why not think they will always escape the judgment of God? Paul says they too are inexcusable. "God will render to every man according to his deeds."

37

Now, here is the next bit of false reasoning. This group declares that they don't know enough to be condemned. They don't know the law of God so how can they be condemned for disobeying what they don't know?

Paul answers the question in verse 12: God "will punish sin wherever it is found. He will punish the heathen when they sin, even though they never had God's written laws, for down in their hearts they know right from wrong." (LNT).

Ignorance is no excuse either. No one will escape if he insists on trying to get along without Christ. "The day will surely come when at God's command Jesus Christ will judge the secret lives of everyone, their inmost thoughts and motives; this is all part of God's great plan" (verse 16 LNT).

Oftentimes we forget the judgment side of the gospel story. For further consideration, look up the word "judgment" in a concordance. Check the New Testament references. Jot down each new concept as you read the passages. What conclusion do you reach as a result of what you have read?

4th Day   God's Chosen Ones   Romans 3:1–8

Paul knew that the Jews considered themselves to be pretty special people. So, in this section of his writing about judgment for sin, he had something to say to the Jews. It was just right for them, and it is just right for anyone who thinks he is pretty special in the eyes of God.

With the idea of being special can come a bit of fallacious reasoning. Summed up it is this: "Since I am someone special, God will not condemn me. In fact the more I sin the more God can show His grace by overlooking it." (See verse 5.)

This dodge will not work any better than the others we have considered. Paul says, in verse 8: "If you follow through with that idea you come to this: the worse we are, the better God likes it!" *(LNT)*.

It is as though the individual forgets that God is holy and just. But forgetting does not change the truth. God is holy and so will not accept anything less than perfection. Any infraction or omission of the commands of God is sin and sin must be judged. There is nothing else that can be done. To overlook it is not possible in light of the holiness of God.

That's a dark picture—except for one thing. Our holy God is merciful. He provided a way whereby sin could be judged and the sinner forgiven. That way is Christ. When a sinner turns to the Lord Jesus and receives Him as his Saviour, the sin of that person is judged in Christ and the sinner forgiven. If any individual refuses God's provision, the sin is judged in the individual and he is condemned. It is as definite and irrevocable as that. Sin must be judged! Each person may choose who will bear the judgment of his sin.

The people Paul wrote about in our Scripture passage disregarded these truths. But their ignorance did not change their status.

Who bears your sin—do you or does Christ?

For further consideration, read John 3:1–21, 31–36. How do these words of the Lord Jesus and about Him bear out the necessity for looking to Christ for forgiveness? According to these verses what is the alternative to receiving Christ?

Paul had never been to Rome when he wrote this letter. There were so many things he wanted to be sure the people knew, that the words seem almost to tumble over each other. He started off—after a few pleasantries—by telling the people that the gospel of Christ was his theme. Then, we picked up through our reading the fact that the world was guilty before God. Look back over the readings for this week and see how he made his point, emphasized it and then reemphasized it.

Now, in the Scripture which we read today he seems to be summarizing the teaching. He had said atheists are guilty, the self-righteous are guilty, the ignorant are guilty, the chosen ones are guilty, and now the truth: All are guilty and are under the penalty of impending judgment of God.

The summary is not easy to take. Paul turned his attention to the Old Testament and gave quote after quote to show that there is nothing in any man to make him good material for smugness. He spoke of almost every part of a person and showed from the Scriptures that man has nothing to make him proud when he faces his God.

These verses would be a mighty dark picture if they were the end of the story. But the glorious message of the Scriptures is that they are not. Alone we are hopeless and helpless, but the Lord did not leave us that way.

Over a couple of chapters Paul wrote: "God showed His great love for us by sending Christ to die for us while we were still sinners. And since by His blood

He did all this for us as sinners, how much more will He do for us now that He has declared us not guilty? Now He will save us from all of God's wrath to come. And since, when we were His enemies, we were brought back to God by the death of His Son, what blessings He must have for us now that we are His friends, and He is living within us! Now we rejoice in our wonderful new relationship with God—all because of what our Lord Jesus Christ has done in dying for our sins—making us friends of God" (Romans 5:8–11, *LNT*).

For further consideration, use a concordance or the marginal references in your Bible and read the passages from the Old Testament which Paul is quoting. You will find that most of the quotes are from Psalms. Read especially Psalm 36. Note that David divides his thoughts into three groups. First, he speaks of the wicked. Then, he praises God for His constant love and mercy and lovingkindness. Finally, David prays. Find the three divisions. What does this psalm say to you and your own relationship to God?

6th Day   The Gift of God   Romans 3:21–26

In this passage Paul turns from the dark picture of our complete failure before God and gives us God's remedy for sin. Fortunately for us one of the words Paul uses is the word "freely" or "as a gift." When the Law was given and our relationship with God depended on our obedience, we failed. Now God offers us as a gift all we need to be right with God.

Read the passage again carefully and notice the words Paul uses to describe God's gifts. The first one we meet is the word "righteousness." Imagine—a sinner can receive the gift of the righteousness of God. It stands to reason the only way a sinner will be right before God is by receiving His righteousness as a gift. Certainly the sinner will never merit it or achieve it on his own. But God will give it to him when by faith he receives Jesus Christ as his Saviour.

That brings us to the second word: "faith." According to Ephesians 2:8, this too is a gift of God. Faith is really believing what God says because it is God who says it. You look at yourself and realize that you are far from perfect, but God says that He has forgiven you and given you the righteousness of Christ. So, though you cannot understand it, you believe it. That is evidence of your faith in God.

Justified is another of the "gift" words. Again this is an act of God in your behalf. When you receive Jesus Christ, God declares that you are cleansed from all unrighteousness and that you stand before Him cleared from guilt.

"Grace" is the next word. You receive from God love and forgiveness which you do not deserve, but which God desires to give you.

Finally there is the word "redemption." The act of Christ when He died in your place and paid the wage sin required (Romans 6:23). He made it possible for you to receive all the gifts of God through His death and resurrection (Romans 3:25,26).

What a wonderful passage to follow so closely upon those which told of God's judgment of sin and our condemnation as sinners!

For further consideration, use a concordance and look up one or more of the words listed above. How much can you learn about each word by reading the ways it is used in the New Testament? What difference does it make in your life?

7th Day   By Faith   Romans 3:27–31

"Therefore we conclude that a man is justified by faith without the deeds of the law" (verse 28). Is that what you conclude? Think about it for a few minutes and determine what Paul means.

"A man is justified." It is possible for imperfect man to stand unashamed in the presence of God who is holy and just. Do you conclude that this is possible? It is because God declares that He gives the righteousness of Christ to a person who comes and confesses that he is a sinner. He receives Jesus Christ as his Saviour, pleads the blood of Christ to cover his sins and asks God to forgive him. Justification is the work of God. Reread verse 24: "Being justified freely by his grace."

"A man is justified by faith." Do you conclude that? Perhaps if God asked something of us we would feel better. But He doesn't. We have nothing to offer which God will accept as part payment for our sins. We come empty-handed. We throw ourselves on the mercy of God. The works of the law, good deeds we have done, one or two examples of obedience on our part—nothing helps us. God declares us justified; we simply receive His forgiveness.

All of this which we have been reading this week has brought us in a complete circle back to where we started. We began in the Garden of Eden before the Fall of Man when God and man had fellowship together. We followed through the fall, to the warning of sure judgment, to the provision for forgiveness and so back to the possibility of man once more being permitted to talk to and have fellowship with God.

For further consideration, read Genesis 3 and list the things which man lost when he sinned. Use a concordance to find where the Bible tells us that these things were restored or even improved upon by Christ's provision for our salvation.

Sin breaks our fellowship with God. We know this from the teaching of the Scriptures, especially in the passages which we read this week. We know it too from our own experience. When a Christian sins he is most uncomfortable until he comes to Christ and confesses the sin and asks for forgiveness.

In I John 1:5–7 we read this admonition: "GOD IS LIGHT, and no shadow of darkness can exist in him. Consequently, if we were to say that we enjoyed fellowship with him and still went on living in darkness, we should be both telling and living a lie. But if we really are living in the same light in which he eternally exists, then we have true fellowship with each other, and the blood which his Son shed for us keeps us clean from all sin" (Phillips).

Think about those verses. How can you live in the light? What does it mean in practical day by day experiences? When you determine what it means, decide how to achieve this fellowship with God. Then, set about putting your thoughts into action.

Chapter 5

ARE YOU
YOUR BROTHER'S KEEPER?

There is really only one way that sin should be dealt with in our lives. That is, confess it and ask God for forgiveness. It is interesting that the Bible does not record Adam and Eve doing either. That does not mean that they did not do these things, but the Bible does not say they did. When God confronted them with the sin they blamed each other and the serpent. Neither confessed his own sin. And as you read on, there is no prayer given, no word of repentance spoken by either of them.

Could this be a reason that one generation later there is a murder in the family? And the murderer

Bible reading for this week: Genesis 4:1–24.

responds, not with repentance, but with concern for his own safety.

1st Day   More than Sons I John 3:1–3

It is a long way from Genesis to I John. We read in Genesis 5 that Adam "begat a son in his own like-ness, after his image." In I John 3 we read that those who have been born by faith into God's family are the sons of God, and that someday "we shall be like him; for we shall see him as he is."

It is no wonder that the apostle John begins this section of his letter by saying, "See how much our heavenly Father loves us" *(LNT)*. That is really hard to do. We cannot begin to understand how much God loves us. But let's make a try at getting some idea.

First, we will have to realize again that God is holy and that any sin is unacceptable to Him. Remembering that, reread Genesis 4:1–24. Do you begin to realize the gulf that exists between God and sinful man?

God realized it, and He spanned it. He made a way out for anyone who will take it. He didn't have to but He did. Honestly now, wouldn't you be satisfied if that were all He did?

But God was not finished. He not only made a way out; He elevated the repentant sinner to the status of His child. That is so much more than we deserve. Certainly anyone would be grateful for such a gift. How much God must love us!

Still He is not finished. Reread verse 2. If you know Jesus Christ as your Saviour you will be more than a child of God. Adam and Eve disobeyed God so that they might "be as gods" (Genesis 3:5,22). That was not the way to achieve such a status. But in I John 3:2 we read that "we know that, when he shall appear, we shall be like him; for we shall see him as he is."

See how very much our heavenly Father loves us!

What shall we do? Read verse 3. "And everyone who really believes this will try to stay pure because Christ is pure" *(LNT)*.

What do you think it means to "stay pure"? For further consideration, you may want to use a concordance and check what the Bible says about it. When you know what the Lord asks, will you practice it?

2nd Day Whose Child? I John 3:4-10

This is a passage of contrasts. In verse 10 John says that there are two groups of people; the children of God and the children of the devil. The verses which precede this statement give the characteristics of the two groups so that we may classify ourselves.

We sometimes feel that there is no reason for us to look at the "children of the devil" list because that could never describe us. But it might be well for us to note that the people in this group are those who have continued in the same way all their lives. They do not know Christ (verse 6). They live in the same pattern they have always lived (verse 8). They sin and they make a practice of sinning (verses 4,8). That is not a pretty description, but it is the picture of anyone who has done nothing to change.

The child of God? He knows Christ and has asked for Him to take away sin (verses 5,6). He has received new life, he is born again (verse 9). He obeys the commandments of God and does not make it a practice to sin because he abides or stays close to Christ (verses 6,9,10). Instead of sinning he does what is right before God (verse 7).

Perhaps as you read the passage, you realize that you need the Lord to work and continue to work in your life that you may attain to the description of the child of God. Tell the Lord. He is willing to provide you with the strength you need.

Yesterday the accent was on what God has done for us. Today the emphasis is on what God expects of us. In order to get a better idea, use your concordance to find the stress the Lord puts upon obedience.

3rd Day   Your Brother and You
I John 3:11–18

How are you at getting along with other Christians? Not just some other Christians, but other Christians in general? That is a meddling-type question, isn't it? But it is the question that the Scripture passage for today raises.

John gives a series of excuses which Christians sometimes give for not really caring for their brothers in Christ. The first is in verse 12. Excuse: "He's better than I am. How can I love him?" This was Cain's excuse, and a great many people have followed in his train.

The Lord said to Cain, "If thou doest well, shalt thou not be accepted?" (Genesis 4:7) You see Abel was no better than Cain could be. And the same is true for you. That Christian of whom you are jealous—he has no corner on God's favor. The Lord is no respecter of persons. Cain's and your excuse falls apart. Even if you must look up to a fellow Christian, the command is "we should love one another" (I John 3:11).

Skip over to verse 17 and look at this excuse. It is in some ways the opposite of Cain's. Excuse: "I worked hard for what I have, why should I have to give it away."

This is another way of saying that we do not want to look down and love. What you have is by the kindness of God. You are no better than the one with less of the material comforts. God does not love you more than the other fellow. God is still no respecter of persons. The command of God is still the same—"we should love one another."

Look at verses 14 and 15. Once more we have an illustration of one Christian not loving another. This time the excuse is—well, it really isn't much of an excuse. Excuse: "I just don't like him. No reason for it. I just don't." This time it isn't envy ("He's better than I am."). It isn't snobbery ("He's not as good as I am."). The Bible agrees, but then gives a name you may not like. The Bible says it's murder (verse 15). There is not a loophole. Christians are expected to love other Christians.

How are we to love? Verse 18 is the answer. "Little children, let us stop just *saying* we love people; let us *really* love them, and *show* it by our *actions*" (*LNT*).

For further consideration, read 1 Corinthians 13. If possible read from at least one of the newer translations. How can you "translate" these characteristics of love into practical guides for dealing with people—especially other Christians?

4th Day   Tongue Trouble   James 3:1–12

James, the author of our Scripture passage, must have been a practical man. The Holy Spirit used him to tell us some of the most down-to-earth truths about our Christian living. In the portion which we read today James gets down to a real problem with most of us—how does what you say show that you are a Christian?

According to the Scripture there are two points to consider when we discuss this problem. It is true that the sins of the tongue are often deemed to be polite sins. They are not to be compared in our minds with gross sins like murder or adultery. Yet, James makes the point that though the tongue is little, it is powerful. Reread verses 5 and 6. The first point then is that the tongue (or our words) has a great potential for evil. The tongue is not wrong in itself. The problem arises when the controller is improperly motivated. Look at verses 9 and 10.

This reasoning brings us directly to James' remedy. We cannot in our own strength control our tongues. See verse 8. *But*, God can! Since the solution is in proper control, the answer lies in God controlling us in every way—including our tongues.

Before you think you don't need the remedy, read verse 2 again. "If anyone can control his tongue, it proves that he has perfect control over himself in every other way" (*LNT*).

For further consideration, read again Genesis 4. How did Cain sin with his tongue? Put each example into a broad category such as lying, conniving, sarcastic, etc. Does this help you know how to pray about the use of your tongue?

5th Day   The Saviour of the World
I John 4:13–16

We have read about the problem. We know of the temptation and fall in the garden of Eden. We know of the murder which resulted just one generation later. We have read of God's hatred of sin and of our own inability to control our tongues and thus of our inability to satisfy the holiness of God. We are sinners and there is nothing we ourselves can do to change the picture.

Now, in today's reading comes the answer. God sent His Son into the world to be the Saviour of the world. What we cannot do for ourselves, God in His mercy did for us. We are imperfect; God sent Christ the perfect one. We are separated from God; God sent His own Son to bring us back to Him. Sin brings death; God sent Jesus Christ to die in our place. All that we need God has provided in Jesus Christ.

Jesus Christ is God the Son—this we need to know and acknowledge. See verse 15. When we receive God's Son, our Saviour, to be God's remedy for our need, a wonderful thing happens. John repeats the truth three times in the short passage which we read. A union takes place between us and God. He comes into our lives in the person of His Holy Spirit. And we find that we are in Christ secure and loved by God.

The more we read of salvation and what God does for us the more we are made to realize that God must really love us. He did so much more than we could have ever dreamed possible. To forgive us would have been more than we deserve. To identify Himself so completely with us as to dwell in us and allow us to be so completely identified with Him that we live in Him is more than we could ever have dreamed possible. What a wonderful Saviour we have!

For further consideration, read the first chapter of Ephesians. Notice the number of times that Paul says we are "in Christ." Sometimes Paul uses another word for Christ like "the beloved." Notice all that Christians have because they are "in Christ."

6th Day   God's Love and Ours
I John 4:17–21

First, God's love. John wants us to understand how great God's love for us really is. He says you can rest in it. You don't have to be afraid of any coming judgment. You don't have to wonder what's going to happen to you. You don't have to keep your eye on your own inadequacies. You don't have to be worried about your failures. You don't have to chew on your nails for anything. When you know the Lord Jesus Christ as your Saviour you can be sure of Him and of His faithfulness. You are His and He loves you and you can rest in those truths. J. B. Phillips translates verses 17, 18 like this: "So our love for him grows more and more, filling us with complete confidence for the day when he shall judge all men—for we realize that our life in this world is actually his life lived in us. Love contains no fear—indeed fully developed love expels every particle of fear, for fear always contains some of the torture of feeling guilty."

Then, our love. John says that first of all we should realize that our love is just a reflection of God's. "We love him, because he first loved us" (verse 19).

52

Our love should go up to God and out to our fellow men. In fact, John says you can't have one direction without the other. You should not be so "heavenly minded" that you are not aware of the needs of those around you. But then, neither can you be so aware of the problems of the world that you leave God out. The Christian way is a balance of both. As John says, "He who loveth God [should] love his brother also" (verse 21).

For further consideration, read the parable of the good Samaritan in Luke 10:25-37. How do you think this parable illustrates the passage from I John? How do you think you can be a "good Samaritan"?

7th Day   Law and Grace
Romans 7:4-12

Our Scripture passage lists three conditions of an individual. Every person on earth is in one of the three conditions.

Taken chronologically, the first condition is described in verse 9. "I felt fine so long as I did not understand what the law really demanded" (*LNT*). This is the condition of false security. This is trying to play Cain's game. The world is populated with people who are refusing to see their need of a Saviour and are pretending that they are all right as they are.

The second condition is described in verse 11. The guilt ridden individual is pictured this time. He knows that he is a sinner and yet he does nothing about it. He may try to ignore the fact. He may try to find his own remedy. He is honestly miserable. Everyone is wrong, including God and His laws in this person's viewpoint. He is miserable but he refuses to do anything about it.

The last condition is the one described in verse 4. This person has discovered that he is a sinner, he has turned to God for help and now he is a new person in Christ Jesus. This does not mean that his problems are over. It does not mean that he will never face the temptation to sin again. It means that he has an answer for the sin question in his life and the answer is Christ.

Read all of Romans 7 and the first four verses of Romans 8. Look for the problem of sin detailed and illustrated. Look for the answer in Jesus Christ. How do these verses show that no one can be his own master of sin? What does Christ do for the person who comes to Him in faith and receives Him as Saviour?

Read again the story of Cain and Abel in Genesis 4. When we know Jesus Christ as our Saviour we realize that God has forgiven us from our life of sin.

God asked Cain a question: "Where is . . . thy brother?" Cain tried to dodge his responsibility. "Am I my brother's keeper?" he asked God. The Lord did not bother to answer. He did not have to; Cain knew the answer.

As Christians, we know that God has forgiven us. We know that we have fellowship with Him because Christ has cleansed us from all sin. All right, for our own lives the question is settled. Now the question, "Where is your brother?"

"Am I my brother's keeper?" From the reading that we have done this week, the answer is obvious.

So what shall we do about it?

Chapter 6

THE TIME WILL COME

Wickedness and obedience, judgment and provision—this is a chapter of contrasts.

Generations had passed since the occurrences in the Garden of Eden. And through them all the pattern was clearly developing—left to himself, man continued the walk away from God. Man was not evolving into a better person, he was drifting and deliberately walking into paths that took him away from his Creator.

Millenia have passed and we look around at our world. Has the course of human nature improved since the days of Noah? Is man now at last reaching toward

Bible reading for the week: Genesis 6:5–8,13,14; 7:1,4,5; 9:8–13.

55

God? The answer is too obvious—too obvious to comment. The solution is that God still makes provision for our needs.

1st Day   Time? Unknown!   Matthew 24:36–44

One of the most disturbing impressions you get when you read Genesis 6 is the utter disregard of the people of Noah's day for the warning of coming judgment. Then, turn to today's Scripture passage and notice that the Lord is saying that the same thing will be true when He comes again. People will be going about their everyday business, paying no attention to the fact that the Lord is coming. It is "business as usual" as far as most people are concerned.

The Lord says that the disregard of some will not affect the fact: He is coming. He said so and that settles it. The Lord is coming back to earth again.

In Noah's day and in ours the question that must arise is "When?" In Noah's time the day seemed to be delayed. Noah went on building and nothing happened. Today, days and years roll by and nothing happens. But just as surely as the Flood came, so surely will the Lord come again to receive His own children and to judge the wickedness of the world.

When? According to the words of the Lord no one knows when. It stands to reason that the answer must be that no one need know when. Our job? The Lord Himself gives the answer: "Watch therefore; for ye know not what hour your Lord doth come" (Matthew 24:42).

What does it mean to "watch for the Lord's return"? For further consideration, use a concordance and check the New Testament use of the word "watch" to help you. How can you watch?

2nd Day Faithful and Wise
Matthew 24:45–51

In these few verses the Lord has presented a contrast in individuals. First, the wise and faithful servant. He is wise because he does not doubt that his lord will return. The lord in the parable has apparently gone away for a time, but with the assurance that he will return. A wise servant believes his lord.

With this description we can safely say that Noah is wise. God said a flood would come and Noah believed Him.

Our Lord has gone away. He, too, left full assurance that He would return. Are we wise servants according to the definition in this parable?

In the story the servant is called faithful. His lord gave him a job to do: "provide for the needs of the other members of the household." The lord returned and found the servant doing just exactly that. His lord called the servant faithful and he rewarded him.

By this definition Noah was faithful. The Lord gave him a job to do: "build an ark." Noah did as God told him.

Our Lord has given us a job to do. Provide for the needs of those around us. Tell them of Christ. Care for their material needs. When the Lord returns will we be declared faithful?

The contrast is given in the "evil servant." His story is exactly the opposite to that of the first servant. This evil one doubted that the lord would return. He was unwise. He took advantage of the people left under his care. He was unfaithful. The Lord Jesus called him evil. When the lord in the parable returned the servant was punished.

His is not Noah's story. It had better not be ours!

How far do you think our responsibilities go in terms of caring for the needs of others? Does our class fulfill this requirement? If not, what should we do further?

3rd Day   Prepared and Wise
Matthew 25:1-13

Another contrast of people is evident in these verses. Once more the similarity between the parable the Lord told and the times of Noah is evident.

The Lord reported that there were two groups of people. The first he called wise. These women prepared for the coming of the bridegroom. They went to meet him and took provision for a long wait, if the bridegroom so desired. They went about their normal business. When it became late they slept. They simply waited until the cry came that the bridegroom was approaching.

Their wisdom paid off. They had made provision so that whenever he came, they would be ready to meet him.

Noah did the same. God told him to build an ark; he built one. God told him to stock it with provisions; he did. When God said that the time had come to enter the ark, Noah was ready.

We have no idea when the Lord will come. We know His coming is a fact, but we do not know the time. The parallel is obvious. We, too, should be going about our daily tasks. But, when the Lord comes, we, too, should be ready and prepared to meet Him. This time the preparation does not include our responsibility to others, as in the first parable. This time the Lord is emphasizing our personal preparation.

Receiving Christ as your Saviour, that is certainly where preparation begins. Anticipating the Lord's return, that's also a part of being ready. Growing and maturing in Him through the study of His Word, obedience to His will, trusting more and more as you learn to live by faith, all of these enter into your personal preparation. All of these make you prepared and wise.

The other group in the parable are the foolish. Look at them, they are the exact opposite of the wise. You are not like them, are you?

For further consideration, use a concordance or your own knowledge of the Bible and find Scripture which bears out the list of what it means to be personally prepared for the coming of the Lord. Can you add any other points to the list?

4th Day   Useful and Wise
Luke 19:12-27

Once more the contrast between people. First we read of a wise servant who discharged his responsibility to others. Then, of five wise women who were wise in their personal preparation. Now, we come to a wise steward who uses well what God has given him.

According to the natural abilities which each servant had, he was given responsibility and opportunity to use those abilities. The wise steward recognized these opportunities and used them to make other opportunities.

A wise servant knows that his abilities are his by the grace of God. Thus he is a steward of them and has a responsibility to use them to God's glory. A wise servant is in this example a useful steward.

You have also received gifts from God's hand. As you honestly look at yourself you can see what God has given you. Now, be wise and use them in the Lord's service. Just to get you started, consider that your life is a gift from God. What do you do with it? Certainly the first fact to face is that as you yield yourself to God and He becomes your Saviour you have eternal life in Christ. One talent or pound has been multiplied by God and you have a natural life and now eternal life. What else do you have that you can use for the Lord's sake?

The foolish servant—obviously he is the one who does not use what God has given him in opportunities of service. This isn't a picture of you, is it?

Take a few minutes to think about the people in the Bible. How many different natural abilities can you think specific people possessed that they used to God's glory? Such thinking will help you assess your own stewardship.

5th Day   Unto the Lord   Matthew 25:31-40

When you read the account of the Flood in Genesis, you can hardly miss the tender care of God for Noah and his family. He warned them of the coming judgment. He told them how they might escape. He shut them safely inside the ark. Then in Genesis 8:1 we read "And God remembered Noah." One family, eight people and God's constant concern for them and their safety. What a wonderful Lord!

In the Scripture which we read today we have another example of the Lord's concern for His people. In fact, as you read the passage notice how closely the Lord identified Himself with "His brethren." The Lord accounts common needs of people: hunger, thirst, loneliness, poverty. The righteous listened. When the Lord said that these needs were His, they found it hard to comprehend. How could the Lord of glory have needs such as these? The Lord answered: "Inasmuch as ye have done it unto one of the least of these my brethren, ye have done it unto me" (Matthew 25:40).

It is so easy to feel that if we are not an evangelist or a missionary, a preacher or a teacher, we are not really in His service. The Lord did not have that viewpoint. Serve others and you serve Him—when you serve in His name. Do everyday homey things for people for Jesus' sake, and it is as though He were here and you were caring for Him.

What sort of an impression for Christ do you make in your community? What could you do in His name for people in need?

6th Day   The Inevitable   Matthew 25:41–46

There is an awful finality about the words in our Scripture passage. There is something just as final in the account of the Flood. When the door of the ark was shut and the rains began to fall, doom was inevitable.

In all the Bible there are no more chilling words than when God says, "Depart from me." We don't like to read words like these. We don't even like to think about them. It is so much easier for us to think that this particular tomorrow—this day of reckoning will never really come.

As sure as heaven and the reward of the saints, so sure is hell and the punishment for rejection of Christ. It is much more pleasant to think and revel in the love of God. But for God's love to have meaning, God's holiness must be a fact. Sin must be judged, there is no escape. Receive Christ and the judgment passes onto Him. Reject Him and the judgment remains on the sinner.

There is a word in verse 46 that we should notice. It is "everlasting" or "eternal." In the first part of this verse it is describing punishment. In the last part it is describing life. The same word is used in both places. You see the fact of an eternal existence is already decreed. Concerning this we have no choice, we shall exist eternally. Our choice is *where* we shall spend eternity—in heaven with eternal life or in hell with eternal punishment!

You can go no further than to consider your own destiny. When this is settled, what part can you play in bringing your family and friends to know eternal life in Christ?

7th Day   Your Influence   Romans 14:10–19

It would probably have been an easy thing for Noah to have used himself as a measure for determining the extent of everyone's failure. It is just as easy for us to do the same thing. All week we have been reading of certain standards of behavior and attitude. So we make our "yardstick" (usually according to our actions and beliefs) and we go about measuring other Christians.

Paul has two things to say about this attitude. First is in verse 10. "You have no right to criticize your brother or look down on him" (*LNT*). That's pretty definite. Don't use your "yardstick" to measure the spiritual maturity of others. The reason: "Each of us will stand personally before the Judgment Seat of God." You do not answer for anyone else, just yourself. Measuring will be done by God's yardstick, not yours.

The second point is in verse 13: "So don't criticize each other any more. Try instead to live in such a way that you will never make your brother stumble by letting him see you doing something he thinks is wrong" (*LNT*). This is saying, "You must not measure others, but conduct yourself in such a way that if they measure you, you will not be a problem to them."

There is no doubt about it—a Christian has a great responsibility before God for those he may influence. It is all summed up in the last two verses of our passage, verses 18, 19: "If you let Christ be Lord in these affairs, God will be glad; and so will your friends. In this way aim for harmony in the church and try to build each other up" (*LNT*).

For further consideration, read 1 Corinthians 8. How does this passage set forth the same points? Read also all of Romans 14. How will the teaching of these chapters affect your daily life?

When the Flood was over and Noah and his family were again on dry ground, they thanked God for His care over them. God was pleased with Noah and his offering. The Lord made a covenant saying that He would never again destroy the world with a flood. Then the Lord set a rainbow in the sky and said that this was a symbol of His covenant. Read Genesis 9:13–17. The rainbow says to us that God still remembers and keeps His Word.

As you read the Scripture this week, you must have faced up to some things the Lord wants you to do. Will you be faithful in your covenant with Him? Perhaps it would help to have a symbol. How about writing out your decisions and putting them in your Bible to remind you of your promise. You may want to go back to the page in this book that has the Scripture passage that made a difference and sign that page with your name and the date.

God is faithful to you. You keep your word to Him!

Chapter 7

LOOK OUT FOR NUMBER 1!

There once were some people who were afraid of losing their identity. They knew that they were supposed to move out and scatter over the countryside, but they felt that they would be lost in a vast world and no one would hear of them again. Their solution was to disregard the command to scatter and to do something which would preserve their identity and make people aware of them.

Does that sound familiar? In one way or another it tells the frustrations of many today. The story, however, is not new. It was enacted on the plains of Shinar in ancient Mesopotamia. It is probably being reenacted somewhere today. Don't you be the leading character.

Bible reading for this week: Genesis 11:1-9.

1st Day   How Much Is Enough?
Luke 12:13–21

The people on the plains of Shinar wanted to make a name for themselves and their desire became an obsession that ruined them.

The rich man in the parable Jesus told wanted wealth and the security he felt would be the natural outgrowth. He found there was no security in wealth and he lost his life.

It is easy for us to shrug our shoulders and dismiss both of these accounts. After all, we are not obsessed with a desire to be famous. We would just as soon be lost in the crowd. But did you ever think that being a nonentity can also be an obsession?

And money—that's no problem. You don't have enough to make a difference. It isn't how much you have that makes the difference, it's what you do with what you have.

The rich man would not have been satisfied if he possessed the world. That was his problem. He announced that already he had "much goods laid up for many years," but that didn't stop him from deciding to build still bigger barns. To possess much wealth was the goal and the pride of his life.

The opposite can be just as true. To possess nothing and still get along can be the goal and pride of a person's life.

These attitudes are not bad in themselves. The problem arises when they become too important and God is crowded out.

The Lord summed up the parable this way: " ' "This very night your life is being demanded; and as for all that you have prepared—who will have it?"

" 'So it is with those who lay by wealth for themselves and are not rich to the glory of God.' "°

For further consideration, read Luke 12:22–34. Find additional teaching of the Lord Jesus with regard to accumulation of material things. Do you think the Lord is condemning providing for our needs?

How do you lay up treasure in heaven?

2nd Day   "Look Me Over!"   Amos 6:8–14

In the days of Amos' prophecy the people of Israel were getting along very well. Times were prosperous, no major wars—all was secure. At least that's what they thought. Then onto the scene came this gatherer of sycamore fruit talking about trouble and judgment. No one listened, no one cared. "It can't happen here," was the byword.

The opening verses of Amos 6 are descriptive of the attitude of the people. Then comes the passage we read today. The Lord warns the people again that their sin will not go unpunished. The sin which He specifically mentions is that of pride. Verse 8: "I despise the pride and false glory of Israel" (*Living Prophecies*).

There is a similarity between Israel in the days of Amos and our affluent society. It probably sounded as strange to the ears of the Israelites to hear that their security was threatened as it would sound to us. But the Lord said that their feeling of security in their own abilities and achievements was foolish. He said it like this in verses 12 and 13: "Can horses run on

°Luke 12:20,21, *The Twentieth Century New Testament* (Chicago: Moody Press). Used by permission.

rocks? Can oxen plow the sea? Stupid even to ask, but no more stupid than what you do when you make a mockery of justice, and corrupt and sour all that should be good and right. And just as stupid is your rejoicing in how great you are, when you are less than nothing! And priding yourselves on your own tiny power!" (*Living Prophecies*).

Pride in self-achievement on the plains of Shinar was foolishness. Pride in Israel was foolish. And our pride in ourselves and our achievements is just as foolish.

For further consideration, use a Bible concordance to look up the word "pride." What does God say about the pride of man? When is pride acceptable?

3rd Day   The Account Is Settled
Isaiah 14:3-15

The king of Babylon, Nebuchadnezzar, was a proud man. The experiences of Daniel bear this out. The last three verses of our Scripture passage tell us the extent to which his pride took him.

It was difficult for the Israelites to see such disregard for God apparently prosper. The people of Israel had sinned, that was true. But they did know the Lord God. Babylon, on the other hand, was a pagan country. Yet Babylon was obviously more powerful than the land of Israel. It must have appeared that sin was going to triumph. Nothing seemed able to stop the tide of the Babylonian surge.

This is the setting for the words of our Scripture passage. God is reassuring His people. The day will come when God will settle the account. The king of

Babylon will not always be the winner. The first three verses of the chapter are assurances to the people of Israel that God will remember them and restore them to their land and give them peace. "Then it shall be that when the Lord has given you rest from your toil and misery, from the hard labour which you had to endure, then you will sing a song of contempt to the king of Babylon" (verse 3, *Four Prophets*).

The land will have rest from war: "Now the whole earth lies quietly at peace, and a song is on every lip" (verse 7, *Four Prophets*).

The wickedness of the king of Babylon will be judged. The picture is graphic and terrible. "Your glory is brought down to the underworld with all your sounds of music. A mattress of maggots lies ready . . . to cover you" (verse 11, *Four Prophets*).

God judged and punished the sin of the people who built the Tower of Babel. He promises punishment to the king who rejected Him. Sin will be judged in every instance. But at the same time He promises peace and blessing to those who confess their sin to Him and ask for forgiveness.

For further consideration, read Daniel 4. This is the account of Nebuchadnezzar's pride and the judgment of God upon him. Pray for our country and its leaders—that they will recognize the need to give God the glory for our successes and prosperity. Read and meditate upon the teaching of James 1:17.

4th Day   The Heart of Man   Mark 7:14–23

The Lord Jesus was talking to the Pharisees, the religious people who put great stress upon external

appearances. The Lord pointed out some of the loop-
holes the Pharisees had made in their interpretation
of the Law of God. Then, He proceeded to deal with
the questions: Is a man a sinner because he sins? Or,
does he sin because he is a sinner?

The Pharisees would like to say that the first was
the case. Then, they would proceed to say that if by
overt act they could keep from breaking their idea
of the commandments of God they were righteous.

The Lord did not agree. He said that the act was
the product of an evil heart. The building of the Tower
of Babel was just the expression of the people's disregard for the Lord God. So, the Lord said that the
evil acts listed in verses 21, 22, are just the expression
of evil hearts.

We know these things, but we do not always remember them. "If I just hadn't lost my temper," we
say. What we really mean is "If I just hadn't been
so unjustly angry." "If I had just kept my mouth shut,"
we say. Really the problem is, "If I hadn't wanted
to justify my actions, or belittle the other fellow, or
prove my point at someone else's expense."

The Pharisees were trying to purify the river when
the source was polluted. How wonderful that the Lord
knows our needs. He does not just excuse our evil
actions, He makes us new creatures in Him. He does
not just ask us to behave, He asks us to love Him.
He does not just ask us to reform, He says we may
be born again. Salvation is not a code of rules, it is
a relationship with God so that the Spirit of God lives
in us.

For further consideration, read II Corinthians
5:14–21. How do these verses teach the same truths

that Christ spoke in Mark 7, which we have just read? What does God do for us? What does He expect of us?

5th Day   "Blessed Are You!"   Matthew 5:1-10

The Sermon on the Mount and especially the Beatitudes from that sermon are some of the best known of the Lord Jesus' utterances. Read the passage from your favorite version. Then turn to one of the newer translations and read it again.

Notice that the Lord is telling the people the same truths He told them in the passage we read yesterday. It is not just what a person does that marks his character, it is what the person is.

The people who built the Tower of Babel do not fare well when we put these descriptive words of Christ alongside their lives and desires. But before we feel too self-righteous, let's take a look to see how we measure up.

Mr. Phillips in his translation uses the following words to describe the people Christ talks about in the Beatitudes: humble-minded, those who know what sorrow means, those who claim nothing, those who are hungry and thirsty for goodness, the merciful, the utterly sincere, those who make peace, those who suffer persecution for the cause of goodness.

When you place the Lord's life on earth alongside these descriptive words, He measures up to each one. Now, look at the words again with yourself in mind. Is the picture as clear? Alone you can never make it, but with Christ all things are possible. The secret will be in letting Him control your life.

The result of being the kind of person Christ describes is a list of bonuses: The humble-minded receive a kingdom. The sorrowful are given courage and comfort. Those who claim nothing receive an inheritance. The hungry and thirsty are satisfied. The merciful receive mercy. The sincere see God. Those who make peace are called God's children. Those who suffer persecution receive a kingdom.

No matter how hard you try you can never outgive God!

For further consideration, do an honest self-evaluation. Where do you especially need God's help in this list of characteristics? Pray, trust God and work diligently on the places you feel the Lord would have you improve.

6th Day   You and Your Brother
Matthew 5:21–26

For the last two days we have been reading some general instructions regarding our attitude. Now in the section which we read today we come to grips with a specific problem. The problem is a common one—getting along with people.

The Lord gives some instruction on this problem. The only difficulty may be that all of His instruction has to do with what you should do about the problem, not about what the other fellow should do.

Let's take them step by step. First, "Thou shalt not kill." That one is not too hard. You probably have not been overly tempted to murder. Next, don't get angry without cause. That one may be a little harder.

It is interesting that many times our anger is greatest when the cause for it is least logical.

Then, the Lord says that you can't indulge in verbal abuse. Many times a person who would never dream of physical violence will indulge in ruining the other individual by talking about or even to him. Several weeks ago we read that James said the tongue was a little member but that much harm was done by it (James 3:2–9).

Then, the Lord says that when you have wronged a person, you must go to him and ask for forgiveness. He even says that you cannot truly worship God if there is something between you and your brother.

Finally, the Lord says that compromise may be necessary on your part if there is to be peace between the two of you.

The Lord did not outline an easy plan. But He certainly provided us with an excellent one if we really want to get along with people.

For further consideration, read Colossians 3:8–25. This is a section of Scripture in which Paul gives suggestions regarding the behavior of Christians as they deal with others. Read and then list the advice Paul gives. How similar is it to the advice of the Lord Jesus? Plan how you will respond to the suggestions you have read.

7th Day   The Summary of It All
Matthew 5:38–48

More advice from the lips of the Lord Jesus. This time we find two principles of action and then a summary statement.

73

First point: Don't try to take matters into your hands and try to get revenge on the one who has wronged you. This point is in verses 38–42. What the Lord asks is not easy, but He gives us an example. He faced the treatment of His trial, conviction and crucifixion without seeking revenge. "And the chief priests accused him of many things; but he answered nothing. . . . And Pilate asked him again, saying, Answerest thou nothing? Behold how many things they witness against thee. But Jesus yet answered nothing; so that Pilate marvelled" (Mark 15:3–5).

Second point: Love your enemies. See Matthew 5:43–47. To be quiet when we are wrongfully accused is hard, and to love the one who wrongs us is even harder. But the Lord gives us an example of this too. "And when they were come to the place, which is called Calvary, there they crucified him. . . . Then said Jesus, Father, forgive them; for they know not what they do" (Luke 23:33,34).

Are you thinking that the Lord Jesus did it, but then He is God? Look at Acts 7:60. This is the account of the stoning of Stephen, the first Christian martyr. Stephen prayed, "Lord, lay not this sin to their charge." And he died. In the strength which the Lord provides it is possible for us to do what He asks.

The summary: "Be ye therefore perfect, even as your Father which is in heaven is perfect" (Matthew 5:48). This is how the Lord Jesus summed up our getting along with people.

For further consideration, read Romans 12. This is another of the chapters which tells us of God's expectations for Christians. List again the requirements. How do these compare with Christ's words in Matthew 5? Pray about your response.

It is easy for us to dismiss the story of the building of the Tower of Babel with the thought that we are not trying to reach God by worshiping the heavens. We read of the pride of these people and decide that we are not as bad as they were.

Then we turn to the teachings of Christ and we begin to realize that sin is sin in His sight. We do not have to build idol temples to sin against Him. We read of His commandments regarding our actions and somehow we become silent—we have not achieved what we should.

Now we can respond in two ways. We can throw up our hands and say, "It's hopeless. I'll never make it. Why bother to try?" That's the easy way. It is also the coward's way.

We can recognize that in ourselves it is hopeless, we cannot control ourselves. But we are not our own, we belong to Jesus Christ. He can accomplish all that He asks of us.

Look at the lists that you made in connection with the last two Scripture passages. What will you do about achieving God's goal for you?

Chapter 8

ALONE? NOT REALLY

Our Scripture this week reminds us of one of the best-known Bible heroes. Abraham, the man who met God and learned that God and His promises are reliable—is the central figure of our concern.

He came from the land of Ur, not far from the plains of Shinar. He traveled to the Land of Promise, Canaan. He received the promise and then waited and waited for God to work. He faced the unknown land, made first-time decisions, endured long waits, met head-on one of the most difficult tests God could give an individual, and emerged as the man of faith—the synonym

Bible reading for this week: Genesis 12:1-3,7; 22:1-8.

for trust. He was the first man to walk this path, but he never walked it alone! Neither will you!

1st Day   The Secret   Hebrews 11:8-12

There is a word that runs like a refrain through all the Scripture which we read this week. The word is "faith." We can hardly think of Abraham without that word coming into our minds.

We know that faith is one of the most important requirements in Scripture. We are born again by grace through faith. We walk by faith. Knowing all this we can learn from Abraham what it means to have faith in God.

Today in the verses which we read we can discover three examples of his faith. The first is told in verse 8. Here it is the faith to move when God commands. To appreciate this we should remember that people were not transients in Abraham's day. Travel was not undertaken without a good cause. Abraham lived in a big city called Ur, not far from the plains of Shinar where the Tower of Babel had been started. For generations his family had lived in this place. Now God was asking him to leave the security of his homeland—Abraham did not even know where he was to go. But he went.

In verse 9 we read that Abraham had faith to stay when God commanded. He stayed in this strange land about one thousand miles from Ur. Abraham had always lived in a house in a city. Now he was living in tents in a country which was almost devoid of cities. Certainly there was nothing there that could be compared with Ur. Now this certainly must have been an additional loss of security. Think what a change this was for Sarah. But both Abraham and Sarah knew it was the Lord's will for them and they obeyed Him and lived in tents.

The third example is in verse 11. More than anything else Abraham and Sarah wished for a son. Years went by and they must have almost lost hope. There was only one ray of hope, God had promised them a son and they trusted Him. Finally Isaac was born. What a change that must have brought into their home. Imagine two older people with a baby in the house. The security of maturity was threatened, but it was God's will and they thanked Him.

How is your security? Will you let it be threatened by obedience to God's will? If you live by faith you will!

For further consideration, reread Genesis 12:1-9. What do you think it meant to Abraham to obey God? Try to imagine his way of life and how it changed. would you follow God at such a cost?

2nd Day   Hardest of All!
Hebrews 11:17-19

Suppose you had waited twenty-five years for something you wanted more than anything in the world. Finally you got what you wanted, and it was everything you had dreamed. Could you give it to God and relinquish all your rights to it?

That is exactly what God asked of Abraham. Then to add to the difficulty, what the Lord wanted was Abraham's son, Isaac. Granted Abraham had God's promise that Isaac would receive the promise of God and that through him He would fulfill the covenant He made with Abraham. But if you were Abraham would you believe that God would do as He promised? Would the thought cross your mind that maybe you were wrong and that Isaac was not the promised heir? Would you think that you must be misunderstanding God? Surely He could not really want you to sacrifice your son.

Would you try to justify yourself by rationalizing that God had never before asked for a human sacrifice, so He probably did not really want one now? In other words, would you have done anything as difficult as what God asked of Abraham? And would you have done it just because God asked it?

Abraham did. That's one of the things that makes him a man of faith. The writer of Hebrews gives us a little insight into the mind of Abraham. God tested Abraham, and Abraham passed the test. Did you notice that the Bible says that Abraham offered Isaac? As far as Abraham was concerned, when God asked for the life of Isaac, Isaac was already dead. What God wants, Abraham does.

Then, Abraham reasoned that God's word was true. God had said that Isaac was the child of promise; therefore, Isaac *was* the child of promise. God would raise Isaac from the dead. That settled the issue in Abraham's mind and he did what God asked.

God honored his faith and Isaac's life was spared. As for Abraham, he passed the test. He believed God. That's what faith really is.

For further consideration, read Genesis 22:1–14. How many points can you find in this chapter which show you that Abraham was a man of faith? Look for evidences where by action or word he accepted the command of God and trusted in His promises.

3rd Day   Deposited to an Account
Romans 4:1-8

In this passage the Lord chooses to tell us more of the faith of Abraham. This time we are given to understand that the fact that Abraham left Ur, or lived in the Land of Promise, or waited for a son, or offered the son to God, were not what made Abraham a man of faith. These were simply tangible evidences that he was a man of faith. We can't see faith so we know of its existence only by watching how the faith shows in the life of the individual.

There is another subtle point in this passage. It is not just the fact that Abraham believed what God told him that showed his faith. To believe what he heard would have seemed foolish to anyone. We have already looked at what God said this week. And we must admit that Abraham might easily have talked himself out of obedience if he had thought only of what God said.

The secret is in verse 3. "Abraham believed God." It was not what Abraham did. It was not even what God said. Abraham was a man of faith because he believed in a Person. God said this trust in Him was "counted unto him for righteousness." That's a good banking term. Abraham believed God and God deposited the trust to Abraham's account as righteousness.

When you think about it, we have much in common with Abraham. Christianity isn't a matter of a handful of rules to obey or a barrelful of sins to shun. Christianity is the relationship between a person and Christ.

You are a Christian when you place your trust in Christ. He accepts you, not your works—good or bad—you. You receive Him! It is as simple and as easy to understand as that.

One of the ways Christ expressed this concept of the relationship between Himself and the individual, was to command, "Follow Me." Not His rules, but Him. For further consideration, use a concordance and check the times that Christ gave this invitation. What do you think following Christ really means?

4th Day   Not Who You Are!
Romans 4:9–12

In verse 8 we read, "Blessed is the man to whom the Lord will not impute sin." The word used for "impute" is the same as in verse 3 where it is translated "counted." In other words, Paul is saying that when God does not put sin to your account, but instead puts righteousness, you are blessed or happy.

Now in the Scripture which we read today Paul goes on to tell us how we receive this "blessedness." Today's Scripture says that we do not receive it because of who we are.

Paul uses the word "circumcision" to mean the Jews. From the days of Abraham to the present day it "has always been regarded as the supreme obligatory sign of loyalty and adherence to Judaism."

The Jews, because of their covenant relationship with God through Abraham, have considered themselves specially honored and above all other people with regard to the worship of the Lord. What Paul says in these verses in Romans is therefore a shock.

The blessing of God, as described in verse 8, is not given on the basis of an individual's nationality.

How do these words affect us today? The application is simple. We do not receive the blessing of being forgiven because we have been born in a certain country. We do not receive God's gift because we have parents or ancestors who once received God's promise. It is not a matter of who we are—that we live in a Christian country, that we have relatives who are Christians. Each person comes just as he is, without any special privileges, and receives from God the gift of forgiveness and cleansing from all sin.

Look again at verse 11. See the phrase, "Those who believe." Look back at verse 3. Believe God! There it is again; salvation is the relationship between God and you—one to one. "That righteousness might be imputed unto them also." The gift of God by faith in Him!

For further consideration, read Matthew 11:28-30. This is the Lord's invitation. To whom is it given? What is the promise? What do you think this "yoke" is? (A Bible dictionary may help you.) What are you to do after taking the yoke? What will be the result? Have you found these things to be true in your life? Perhaps you would like to share your experience with someone.

5th Day "Not What You Do!"
Romans 4:13-15

These verses are a continuation of what we read yesterday. They present for us the second point about the blessing spoken of in verse 8. This time Paul tells us that we do not receive the blessing based on what we do.

To understand what Paul is saying we should look once again at the Jews who first read his words. Throughout their history the Jews proudly proclaimed themselves to be the "People of the Book." By this they meant that the Law of God, the words of the prophets—in short, the Old Testament—was given to them. They were the custodians of the Scriptures.

The interpretation of the Scriptures and the codifying of the laws occupied the time of the great Jewish scholars. The school became the most important place in the community. The piety of an individual was measured by the number of hours he spent each day in reading and meditating upon the Scriptures of the Old Testament.

Now reread the verses from Romans. Do you see how shocking they were? Righteousness was not a matter of keeping the Law but was rather a gift of God by faith in Him.

Before we dismiss the words as not applying to us, consider—do we judge the spirituality of a person by how well he follows our list of taboos, or by his relationship with Jesus Christ?

The blessing of forgiveness and cleansing is not based on what you do but on your relationship with a Person, the Lord Jesus. There is the truth again. Life is in Christ and only in Him. Obedience follows, but can never precede your knowing Christ.

For further consideration, read John 5:30–47. How do these words of Christ bear out what we read in Romans? How can you paraphrase the words of Christ so that you can better understand their meaning? Check other translations for help.

6th Day   "By Faith in Christ"
Romans 4:16–25

At last Paul gets to the positive answer to the question in verse 10. How does this blessing come to us? We have read that forgiveness is not based on who we are or what we do. How does it come to us? By faith in Christ Jesus. Verse 16 begins: "Therefore it is of faith, that it might be by grace."

That is quite a phrase when you think about it. You become a Christian by receiving God's gift. You do not earn the gift. You do not deserve it. You do not do anything to get it. You simply receive it, freely. That is what grace is, an undeserved gift. If you did anything to obtain this grace it would no longer be a true gift. There is a gospel song which says, "Just as I am . . . I come!" Simply because God invites you, that's what the song says: "Thou bidd'st me come to Thee." Another song says, "Nothing in my hands I bring." That may be hard to admit, but it is true. You bring nothing to God to trade, to the smallest degree, for His salvation.

The gift of the grace of God is applied by means of faith. You believe God and trust that He has forgiven you and cleansed you from your sin. He does it because Jesus Christ died for you and rose again from the dead (verses 24,25).

Abraham believed God. You believe God. You find that God puts the righteousness of Christ to your account (verses 22–24). Your salvation then is "of faith, that it might be by grace."

Since salvation is by the grace of God, how do works fit into God's plan for us? Remembering that good works cannot save you, do you think evil works will condemn you? What can you find in the Scriptures to substantiate your answer?

7th Day   The Gift of God   Romans 5:1-11

Paul has made his point. We receive the blessing of forgiveness by faith. Now, in this section he goes into detail to tell us what this blessing includes.

First, the fact that we are justified. This word is another way of saying that God has given us the righteousness of Christ. Look again at Romans 4:22–25. Sin is not placed to our account, but instead, righteousness. Christ took our sin and gives us His righteousness. This does not mean that we immediately become sinless, but it does mean that God declares that the Law has been satisfied and we do not pay the penalty for breaking it.

When we really comprehend all that this gift of God means it is logical that we have "peace with God" (verse 1). And Paul says that this peace is the result of our being justified. After all, if God has given us the righteousness of Christ we can be sure that His righteousness is all that God requires. What have we to fear?

In verse 2 Paul says that since we are justified we have entered into a new relationship with God. He is our Father and we know that having trusted Him to take care of our past shortcomings we can trust Him with our present life and our future destiny. J. B. Phillips translates the verse like this: "Through him we have confidently entered into this new relationship of grace, and here we take our stand, in happy certainty of the glorious things he has for us in the future."

The list goes on and on as Paul thinks of what Christ has done for us who have received Him as our Saviour. Finally, Paul comes to the place where he must admit that he really does not know all that the Lord will do. Since the Lord did so much for us before we ever knew Him Paul says: "What blessings He must have for us now that we are His friends, and He is living within us!" (verse 10, *LNT*).

For further consideration, read Ephesians 2:1–13. This is another of the passages in which Paul details what it means to know Christ as Saviour. What gifts of God do you find enumerated in these verses? Are you beginning to see what it means to be justified by God?

Read again the introductory Scriptures listed at the beginning to this chapter. When we consider Abraham and God's goodness in calling him, and then turn to the New Testament and read how much more we have in Jesus Christ, is there any other logical response than one of gratitude to God for His gifts to us?

Paul thought of all that God had done and prayed for the people. Read his prayer in Colossians 1:9–14. Would you like this to be true for you? Then pray the prayer and diligently seek the will of God through the study of His Word.

Chapter 9

WHAT REALLY COUNTS?

Abraham and Lot were products of the same family, the same environment, the same comparatively easy way of life. What really made the difference between them?

When you take a good look at their lives and the decisions they made throughout their lives, one point comes clearly into view. The difference between these two men was in the matter of their values. Each man looked at a similar circumstance but found a different reason for his actions.

Last week we looked at Abraham and his response to his circumstances. This week we turn to Lot. As you read the introductory Scriptures, consider why Lot acted as he did.

Bible reading for this week: Genesis 13:8–13; 18:20–22; 19:24–29.

1st Day   One of the Crowd
I Corinthians 10:1–5

Abraham left Ur and headed for Haran and Lot went with him. Abraham left Haran and went to the land God promised to give him. Lot went with him. Abraham built an altar and worshiped God at Shechem. Lot watched. Abraham came to Bethel and built another altar. Lot saw this too. Somehow as long as Abraham and Lot were together, Lot got along all right. But just being in the company of Abraham was not enough. Lot had to assume the responsibility for himself and his family.

In today's Scripture we read of the Israelites who traveled with Moses through the wilderness. Notice the word "all" in the verses. *All* our fathers were under the cloud. *All* passed through the Red Sea. *All* drank of the water God provided. *All* ate the manna. *All* were identified with Moses.

Now read verse 5. "But with many of them God was not well pleased." Just being with Moses and even being a part of the miracles which God performed for them, was not enough.

That's enough to make you stop and think. Are you just one of the crowd, or are you one whose relationship with Christ is personal? When you think about it like that, you want to get off by yourself and take a good look at yourself. Better yet, look at yourself as God sees you. If you are a Christian He sees you in Christ. If you are not, you are just one of the crowd who associates with Christians and with their Lord.

For further consideration, read Genesis 13. What were Lot's mistakes? How could he have changed his circumstances? What can you learn from Lot's mistakes? What kind of an application can you make in your daily experiences?

2nd Day   "I Can Take It!"
I Corinthians 10:6–13

Lot faced the city of Sodom. He must have known of its wickedness, but apparently his feeling was, "I can take it!" He didn't do too well. Association with the sinful city lost him his home, his wife, several members of his family. Even the two daughters who survived were hardly worth mentioning.

In our Scripture passage for today, it might well be that the Israelites felt, "We can take it!" But they could not, and they failed.

What of us? According to what Paul says in these verses, there is one sense in which we can take it and one in which we cannot. Is that confusing?

Look at verse 12. This verse gives the attitude that Lot and the Israelites shared. It is the sense in which we are sure to fail. Mr. Phillips translates the verse this way: "So let the man who feels sure of his standing today be careful that he does not fall tomorrow." If we feel we are strong enough to meet temptation head-on, and in our own strength withstand it, we are no doubt already on the way to failure.

Now, look at verse 13. This is the secret which enables us to say, "I can take it," and be right. Read it in your Bible and then let's turn again to Mr. Phillips: "No temptation has come your way that is too hard for flesh and blood to bear. But God can be trusted not to allow you to suffer any temptation beyond your power of endurance. He will see to it that every temptation has a way out, so that it will never be impossible for you to bear it."

In your own strength—failure! In the strength the Lord provides—you can take it! Did you notice Paul did not say you would escape the temptation, only that you could bear it.

For further consideration, make a list of the possibilities for failure in your life at the present time. Now, can you find the "way out" that God says He provides? Make your list your prayer reminder that God will give you the strength to resist the temptations and bear up under the difficulties.

3rd Day   A Foot on Each Side
I Corinthians 10:14–22

Once again there is a parallel between the life of Lot and the words of Paul. Certainly Lot did not start out intending to lead his family away from the Lord. He had spent enough time with Abraham that we can be fairly certain he wanted to follow the ways of Abraham. He certainly knew of God's promise to Abraham and he knew of the worship of God. Lot's problem arose from the fact that he thought he could have Sodom and God too. With Lot it was sort of a foot on each side of the fence.

Then when we read the words of Paul, we find that he is describing the same sort of involvement. The people in Corinth to whom Paul was writing wanted to be Christians and take part in the worship of Christ, but they also wanted to have some tie with those who had nothing to do with Christ. In fact, Paul says these others were really devil worshipers. In all probability the Christians in Corinth had no idea that they were involved in anything as satanic as devil worship. All the Corinthians wanted was to stand with a foot on each side of the fence.

In our complicated world with all the problems of survival and the extra leisure we are afforded, it is not popular to talk about a Christian being different from those who have nothing to do with their Lord. We can so easily compromise and feel that in order to get along in this world we have to have one foot on each side of the fence.

Paul says in verse 22: "Are we trying to arouse the wrath of God? Have we forgotten how completely we are in his hands?" (Phillips) Well, have we?

If you really took the verses in I Corinthians seriously, what difference would it make in your life? Are you ready to accept the difference? If not, what is holding you back?

4th Day   The Law That Governs
I Corinthians 10:23-33

One of Abraham's remarkable attitudes is seen in the way he treated Lot. Apparently Abraham felt a responsibility for his nephew and he could never quite divorce himself from that responsibility. When Lot was captured by a foreign army, Abraham went to rescue him. (See Genesis 14.) When Abraham learned that Sodom was to be destroyed for its sin he interceded in Lot's behalf to have the city spared. (See Genesis 18.) Somehow Lot always seemed to be Abraham's responsibility.

When we turn to I Corinthians we discover that

Paul spoke about this responsibility of one Christian for another. The section which we read today brings out most clearly that a Christian is to conduct himself according to the influence that his life may have on another. Notice that Paul said that the reason for this concern was not based on a you-have-to-or-else law, but instead was based upon the Christian's love for a brother in Christ.

In Paul's day the problem was often the eating or not eating of meat that had been used in the worship of idols. Paul used this problem as an illustration of the way a Christian should conduct himself. He says that a Christian should be willing to forego meat that had been used in this way if the eating of it would be a problem to others. The Corinthians asked why they should change their way of living and Paul answered, "Because, whatever you do, eating or drinking or anything else, everything should be done to bring glory to God" (verse 31, Phillips).

In our day the problem may be entirely different but the answer is still the same. Because you love God and your brother you will govern your decision by the criterion, "Will God be honored by what I do?"

For further consideration, read I Corinthians 8. In this chapter Paul uses the same illustration, the eating of meat sacrificed to idols, to discuss how a Christian should conduct himself. What additional guides do you find in this passage?

5th Day   Lukewarm!   Revelation 3:14–22

When you think about it, there is hardly anything that we like lukewarm. Foods are not pleasing unless they are either hot or cold. Lukewarm soup or luke-warm orange juice is not exactly a gourmet's delight.

The problem that Lucy sees with Charlie Brown in the "Peanuts" comic strip is that he is so wishy-washy.

The individual who can be swayed by every breeze of discussion that blows is the yes-man we constantly belittle.

When it comes to spiritual matters the problem is just as obvious. The Scriptures are filled with illustrations and admonitions against such a person. Lot, whom we have been considering all week, is an excellent example of the man who blows hot and cold. His environment so influenced his actions that he could never be depended upon to stand for anything.

The Scripture we read today tells of the church at Laodicea, another example of lukewarmness. And Christ stands at the door and knocks and waits for an invitation to come in and fellowship with them.

James warns in his letter: "The man who trusts God, but with inward reservations, is like a wave of the sea, carried forward by the wind one moment and driven back the next. That sort of man cannot hope to receive anything from the Lord, and the life of a man of divided loyalty will reveal instability at every turn" (James 1:6–8, Phillips).

The opposite type of person is also described: "And so, brothers of mine, stand firm! Let nothing move you as you busy yourselves in the Lord's work. Be sure that nothing you do for him is ever lost or ever wasted" (I Corinthians 15:58, Phillips).

How do you achieve the steadfastness that God requires? After you have thought about the question turn to Matthew 7:24-27. Does this passage speak to the problem? How?

6th Day   Mean What You Say
II Corinthians 1:15-22

All this talk of compromise and of being luke-warm—neither hot nor cold in conviction, does this mean we can never change our minds? Apparently this is the question that the apostle Paul set out to answer in the Scripture we read today.

Paul had told the Corinthian Christians that he would come to see them. He says in this passage that he planned to visit Corinth twice on this trip through Europe. Paul had planned to go to Corinth on his way from Ephesus to Macedonia and then to revisit them when he was on his way to Jerusalem. But the Lord led differently and Paul did not get to Corinth at all. Paul was anxious that the people know that he had not made a false promise, but that he had instead been made to change his mind when the Lord led him in different ways.

Mr. Phillips makes this point clear when he translates verses 17-22: "Because we had to change this plan, does it mean that we are fickle? Do you think I plan with my tongue in my cheek, saying 'yes' and meaning 'no'? . . . Jesus Christ, the Son of God, whom Silvanus, Timothy and I have preached to you is him-self no doubtful quantity, he is the divine 'Yes.' Every promise of God finds its affirmative in him, and through him can be said the final amen, to the glory of God. We owe our position in Christ to this God of positive promise: it is he who has consecrated us to this special

work, he who has given us the living guarantee of
the Spirit in our hearts. Are we then the men to say
one thing and mean another?"

How about you? Can you accept a change in your
plans when the Lord leads you? Can you accept disap-
pointments when they come?

For further consideration, read Psalm 63. Notice that
the psalm covers a day in David's life. It begins with
morning and proceeds to evening. What can you find
in this psalm that will help you accept the leading
of the Lord even when your plans are changed?

7th Day   "The Lord Knoweth How . . ."
II Peter 2:4–10

It is a wonderfully comforting situation to be able
to leave the problem of judgment to God. It is good
to know that our God is sovereign and that He can
and will take care of the judgment of sin in this world.
It is good to let God be God!

Peter outlined times when God took care of flagrant
disobedience in the world. He used three illustrations:
One was judgment of angels, one judgment of world,
one judgment of particular places. It seems that Peter
may be saying, God will judge any eventuality. Don't
you be concerned, God will judge righteously. "The
Lord knoweth how. . .to reserve the unjust unto the
day of judgment to be punished."

Then, having made that point clear, Peter turned
to the opposite side: "The Lord knoweth how to deliver the godly out of temptation." There appears to be
just two groups of people in Peter's mind. There are
those who refuse to obey God and so will have to

receive His judgment on their sins. There are those who belong to the Lord and can trust Him to deliver them from falling under the temptation that brings disobedience.

For further consideration, read I John 5:10–21. The Lord knows how to take care of His children. And with His gracious concern He says there are some things we may know. Look for these as you read the Scripture. What does this knowledge mean to you?

Did you notice that in the passage from II Peter Lot was referred to as "just" and "righteous"? Does it surprise you to find those words used about Lot? Remember the Lord looks on the hearts of men. He knows the thoughts and the motives behind what each one of us does. He knew Lot and He knew his character.

We would probably never think to apply those words to the man who was guilty of so much compromise, to the one who found his home in wicked Sodom. We are wrong in condemning Lot's stand before God. We judge by the outward appearances. But what a sad commentary on Lot's life that we do not know of his concern when he saw the sin of Sodom. We do not know how he felt in the midst of the immorality in which he lived. The influence of his life is lost to us—perhaps lost to his contempories.

When others watch your life do they know of your love for God and for them? Do they see your concern for those who do not know your Lord? Or, are you more like Lot?

Chapter 10

THE BETTER PART OF VALOR

All three of the patriarchs in the Old Testament are men of varied personalities. Abraham is the man of quiet strength and faithful obedience to God's word. Isaac is the man of quiet acquiescence to his surroundings. Jacob is hardly quiet about anything. But certainly he represents another of the men of strength who through hardship learned to obey God.

This week we look at the man in the middle, Isaac. We know the least about him, and even in the accounts in which he figures, others are often more important. His sacrifice on Mount Moriah accents his father Abraham. The procuring of a bride centers around the

Bible reading for this week: Genesis 26:17-29.

97

servant sent to get her. This passage is the one instance in which Isaac stands in the center of the action.

1st Day   The Promise   Genesis 26:1–5

Do you have a tendency to measure your success in a certain venture by looking to someone else who succeeded and see how you compare? Do you do the same with your relationship to God? It is probably a natural reaction, but not always a wise or valid one in finding the answer.

Isaac was so different from his father. Abraham was a man of action. When there was trouble, Abraham gathered his personal army and went to take care of the problem. Isaac didn't want to fight. He didn't even want to exert his own rights in terms of the wells he had dug. Abraham talked things over with the Lord on a number of occasions. There is just this one record of the Lord coming to Isaac.

Father and son were different, but God used them both. In the passage which we read today God confirmed the promise which He had made to Abraham. He told Isaac that the same covenant was in existence between God and Isaac.

You don't have to be like everyone else to be the recipient of God's goodness. You do not even have to be like the one you consider to be a giant in the faith. God uses you as you are. He loves you as you are. Your responsibility is uniquely yours. You don't have to live anybody's life but your own. The success or failure of every individual rests on whether he responds to God's direction in his life and obediently follows Christ.

Think about the disciples who walked with the Lord Jesus. Consider some of the leaders of the church in Acts. How many different types of individuals and talents did the Lord use for His glory? Read again the accounts of their lives in the Gospels and in Acts.

2nd Day What Do You Want?
James 4:1-3

When you come right down to it, what do you want? Isaac wanted peace. He wanted peace more than he wanted water. James looks at the question and comes up with three answers in three verses.

What do you want? "My own way"? See verse 1. In the language of today we would probably say, "my rights, at any cost." James seems to point out that the problem occurs when what you want springs from "a whole army of evil desires within you" (*LNT*). Sometimes, as unfair as it may sound, you cannot have your rights, unless you are willing for others to be hurt in the process.

What do you want? James says, "What *you* have." See verse 2. "You long for what others have, and can't afford it, so you start a fight to take it away from them" (*LNT*). Again, we might say it in today's language, "Your rights, that's what I want." Obviously this is the one which really causes trouble. When the first individual meets this second one, there is bound to be war. That's what James warns. And that is what Isaac and the Philistines illustrate. If Isaac had wanted his rights as much as the Philistines wanted Isaac's rights, there would have been war between them for sure.

What do you want? "Whatever pleases me at the moment"? See verse 3.

There you have them, the reasons for conflicts. They are the reasonings of an individual who lives for himself alone.

When you come right down to it, what do *you* want?

Think about it. Suppose the Lord Jesus had had this philosophy. Where would we stand?

Suppose Paul had had this philosophy. What would have happened to the early church?

What practical approach could you and your church take to this problem of selfishness?

3rd Day Effective Witness
Genesis 26:17–22, 26–31

If you don't live a showy type of life, it is easy to shortchange yourself. If you do not serve the Lord in some obvious position where you are in front of groups of people, it is easy to wonder what effect your life may have on people in your group.

If this is the way you look at yourself, take a look at Isaac. He is a sort of behind-the-scenes man. If you could have asked him what influence he had for God upon the people around him, he might have shrugged his shoulders and muttered something about "not much I'm afraid," and gone on his way. You see, all Isaac did was refuse to fight for his rights. The ownership of the well meant ownership of the land. It was his land. God had promised it to him. But Isaac was not the type of person to make a point of what was his.

Isaac simply moved on and dug another well. If that was a problem, he moved on again. Now, that doesn't seem like such a remarkable accomplishment, does it? But read on!

The king, the king's friend and the captain of the army came to Isaac. "And they said, We saw certainly that the LORD was with thee" (verse 28).

No, Isaac wasn't spectacular in his relationship to the Lord. He didn't do anything that seems so unusual. But God honored Isaac for doing what he was capable of doing, and the heathen around learned of Isaac's God.

You are what you are because God made you that way. Now be what you are in obedience to the Lord and to His glory.

For further consideration, use a Bible concordance and look up the names "Obadiah" (the servant of Ahab), "Bezaleel," "Aholiab," and "Epaphroditus." Who are these people? What did they do for the Lord? Read also Romans 16. Notice what Paul says about these little-known Christians? Thank the Lord for making you as you are. Ask Him how He can use you for His glory.

4th Day   Who Me?
Romans 12:9–13

As soon as we try to think about non-showy ways to demonstrate our love for Christ we find it hard to be specific. If this has been your problem, today's passage is for you. The list is made up apparently of suggestions which do not require special talent to achieve. And the list is certainly specific.

Look at the verses, slowly, one at a time. *The Living New Testament* translates the list like this: "Don't just pretend that you love others: really love them." It might have been easier if Paul would not have left the door so far open that almost anyone can get in. That word "others" is certainly all-inclusive.

"Hate what is wrong. Stand on the side of the good." Sometimes it seems more interesting to love the wrong. Or, even if we turn from the evil, is it really necessary to take a stand on the good? Couldn't we just be passively neutral? Paul says no.

"Take delight in honoring each other." You mean I am expected to do more than just put up with someone? I'm supposed to let him take precedence over me? That's right!

"Never be lazy in your work, but serve the Lord enthusiastically." But enthusiasm comes and goes. Some days it's easier to serve than others. Paul doesn't leave a loophole.

"Be glad for all God is planning for you." All? Even when I don't understand why I am in the situation I am? Uh huh!

"Be patient in trouble, and prayerful always." Patient—that's going pretty far!

"When God's children are in need, you be the one to help them out."

When you read a list like that you can't help but realize that it takes more grace than you have to achieve it! More grace is available. Ask God for it!

For further consideration, make a list of the characteristics Paul wrote about. Rate yourself—be honest. The rating is between you and God. Now start working diligently on the ones where you need to improve. Take them one at a time. Be sure you look to God for the grace to achieve.

5th Day   There's More?   Romans 12:14–21

The list continues. Let's look at the items from the *Living New Testament* translation: "If someone mistreats you because you are a Christian, don't curse him; pray that God will bless him." You know the best way to lose an enemy is to start praying for him. Before you know it you'll discover that he's not as bad as you thought he was.

"When others are happy, be happy with them. If they are sad, share their sorrow." The first part is not so hard. The second part will take your depending on the Lord for compassion and sympathy.

"Work happily together." Working together, that sometimes is not easy. Do it happily. That is even harder.

"Don't try to get into the good graces of important people, but enjoy the company of ordinary folks." Do you suppose that Paul meant this to include business associations?

"And don't think you know it all!" Even if you do, don't think it. Can you listen as well as talk? That is, listen so that you really know what the other person is saying?

"Do things in such a way that everyone can see you are honest clear through." Are you honest clear through?

"Be at peace with everyone, just as much as possible." Don't quarrel, Paul says. That can be clutching your hands behind your back and clenching your teeth. Be at peace, that's the positive action—more than just not quarreling.

"Never avenge yourselves." Even though it is nice to get even, don't!

103

The summary: "Don't let evil get the upper hand but conquer evil by doing good."

Continue your list from yesterday and also rate yourself on the new items. You will now have more to work on and certainly more to add to your prayer list. You will never make it without God's help.

6th Day   The Broad View   Romans 13:1-10

Now Paul looks beyond the individual with his own problems and considers the individual with regard to those who are in authority. Again, Paul does not give an easy picture. It was not easy when Paul wrote. The land of Israel was under Roman rule and occupation. The leaders of the country were pagan and worshiped the gods of Rome. Even the emperor was considered to be divine. The people who lived in Rome were even more closely bound by the rule of pagan emperors. To these people, and to us, Paul said: "Every Christian ought to obey the civil authorities, for all legitimate authority is derived from God's authority, and the existing authority is appointed under God" (Romans 13:1, Phillips).

Having made this point, Paul went on. The motivating power behind all the behavior that he has been describing is love. When you love your neighbor as yourself you will not "harm or cheat him, or kill him or steal from him" (verse 9, LNT).

Verse 10 summarizes the point: "Love worketh no ill to his neighbour; therefore love is the fulfilling of the law."

Isaac practiced this rule and the rulers of the land recognized that the Lord was with him. Paul practiced this rule and he won some of Caesar's own household to Christ. See Philippians 4:22.

Suppose you practiced it. What do you think the Lord might do in you, for you and through you?

How do you think you could learn to love people in the way Paul described?

Read John 13:31–35. What does Christ say about the business of loving one another? Is it really important? Why?

7th Day   Even if You Are Misunderstood
I Peter 3:8–18

As you read Peter's list of directions, did you feel that he didn't know your circumstances or he wouldn't have written as he did? Verse 14, did that seem to you to be asking too much and perhaps not too realistic? Before you commit yourself, think about Peter for a moment.

He had been in prison on several occasions simply because he was a Christian and obeyed the Lord. The Jews had arrested him (Acts 4). The representative of the Roman government, Herod, had arrested him (Acts 12). Now, Peter was writing to Christians and he was probably in Rome just a few years before his death at the hands of the Romans. Peter knew what he was talking about when he talked about persecution. He might have used himself as an illustration, but he didn't. He chose to use Christ. It is just possible that Peter never really thought about using himself. Over the years Peter had learned that Christ was the center of Christianity and was to be the center of his life.

How can you ever face disappointment or physical or mental turmoil? Listen: "Simply concentrate on being completely devoted to Christ in your hearts. Be ready at any time to give a a quiet and reverent answer to any man who wants a reason for the hope that you have within you" (verse 15, Phillips).

The answer is in Christ. He is the reason for the way you live. He is the answer for how you face the problems of life. Everything is all bound up in your relationship to the Lord Jesus Christ Himself.

What is the hope that is within you? For further consideration, use a Bible concordance and look up the word "hope" as it is used in the New Testament. Remember that hope is not wishful thinking, it is an anticipation for something that you are assured will take place.

You may feel that you are different from other Christians, but that is no problem. You are not called to be like others, you are called to be like Christ.

The Lord faced crowds of people who approved of what He did for them, and the Lord pointed them to His Father.

He faced opposition and adversity and in that circumstance He glorified His Father.

How do you face the good times and the bad? When you are in trouble it is easy to remember to pray. But do you really meet God and respond to Him in such a way that others see the Lord is with you?

When things go well, do you still remember your Lord and your need for fellowship with Him? Can others look at you during the good times and recognize that the Lord is with you?

Chapter 11

THE STRUGGLE

Never were twins less alike than Jacob and Esau. Their physical appearance was so dissimilar that one may not even have recognized them as brothers. Their personalities were direct opposites. Even their sense of values was largely at opposite ends of the pole.

Both had their faults. And both at times in their lives had their victories with virtue. Their stories are told in the Bible without any glossing over. In this chapter and the next we shall take a look at the boys. We shall see their triumphs and failures.

If we are honest we shall look at them and see a reflection of our own personalities. When we do, let's commit ourselves to the Lord afresh.

Bible reading for this week: Genesis 25:21–23, 27–34.

1st Day   Look Around You!
Hebrews 12:12-17

The easiest thing in the world to do is to criticize. And in the case of Isaac's family, we can indulge to our heart's content. We can criticize Isaac for not taking a stand against the underground plots. Rebekah—we can blame her for the conniving she did with Jacob. Jacob wasn't fair with Esau and took advantage of him in a weak moment. Esau should have thought more highly of his birthright. From our vantage point we can see the faults in all of them.

While we are looking the family over and quietly taking them apart, consider this: what would have happened if any one of them had considered someone else? In the passage which we just read the writer of Hebrews says: "Take a new grip with your tired hands, stand firm on your shaky legs, And mark out a straight, smooth path for your feet so that those who follow you, though weak and lame, will not fall and hurt themselves, but become strong" (verses 12, 13, *LNT*).

What would have happened if one member of Isaac's family would have done what those verses describe? Either for himself or for someone else?

What would happen if you took this kind of outlook on the troublesome affairs which come into your life? Verse 15 says: "Look after each other so that not one of you will fail to find God's best blessings. Watch out that no bitterness takes root among you, for as it springs up it causes deep trouble, hurting many in their spiritual lives" (*LNT*).

That is mighty good advice for today!

For further consideration, read Hebrews 12:1-17 in

at least two translations. Look for the correct response to those who watch us, to Christ who leads us, to problems which confront us, to correction which comes upon us.

2nd Day   For and Against
I John 2:12–17.

This particular passage should give us a few minutes of reflection. Notice that John says he is talking to all age groups, children, young people, older folk, everyone is included. The exclusive nature of what he has to say is not a matter of age.

There is one requisite, however, that is the young people John is addressing are Christians only. Notice what he says about each of the age groups. You can readily see that John has only those who know Jesus Christ as their Saviour in mind.

Now read again what he has to say to these Christians. You will find the message beginning with verse 15. Does this mean that Christians may be guilty of "loving the world"? It is hard to deny it in light of what John says.

If, however, we live only in verses 15 and 16, we have only the negative view of staying away from evil. Certainly it is good to stay away from evil, but it is not enough.

Esau fared rather well if all he had to do was have a disregard for the things money and influence can bring. After all he sold his birthright and that is exactly what the birthright included—double portion of his father's wealth and the right to be head of the household.

There is also verse 17, and this is the positive picture for Christians. Not only are we to stop "loving the world" (that is, putting material things first in our lives), but we are also to "do the will of God." This was Esau's downfall. He was against materialism but he forgot to be for the spiritual.

It is so easy for us to be against "worldliness" but forget to be actively for what God wills for us!

How do you really fare with these verses from John? Be honest enough to take a real look at yourself. What are you against? That won't be hard to list. Now, what are you for? What are you doing about these things?

3rd Day   Darkness That Blinds
I John 2:7–11

There is an unusual phrase in the passage that we read today. Did you notice it? We usually talk about light blinding us, but John has chosen to speak of "darkness [that] hath blinded" the individual.

The word John uses for blind has a root meaning "to smoke" or "burn." It is as though the darkness gets into your eyes and you cannot see. Something from the outside is the offender. In John's analogy the irritant is the fact that you do not really love a Christian brother.

These words were written by the man whom the Lord had once called "the son of thunder." John was the one who had wanted to call down fire upon the Samaritans who refused the Lord passage through their land. (See Luke 9:51–56.) But a number of years had passed since the Lord was on earth and John had learned a great many things. In the course of the years the Lord had turned the son of thunder into the apostle of love.

The same commandment concerning the need for Christians to love one another is given to us as well. The Lord Himself said, "By this shall all men know that ye are my disciples, if ye have love one to another" (John 13:35).

If you obey you walk in the light. If you ignore the commandment you will walk in darkness that blinds you. How are you walking? Take care—in the darkness that blinds you may not even realize you are blind.

John says that this is not a new commandment that we love one another. How many times can you find it given in the Scriptures?

4th Day   How Much Do You Care?
Romans 9:1-5

Apparently one of the really difficult things for Paul to accept was that his fellow Jews did not particularly listen to him and they did not as a large group come to know Jesus Christ as their Messiah and Saviour. This passage in Romans is one of the heartfelt outcries of Paul in behalf of his people. "Oh, Israel, my people! Oh, my Jewish brothers! How I long for you to come to Christ. My heart is heavy within me and I grieve bitterly day and night because of you. Christ knows and the Holy Spirit knows that it is no mere pretense when I say that I would be willing to be forever damned if that would save you" (verses 1-3, *LNT*).

Of course there is no way that Paul can decide for anyone. Each person has to make up his own mind whether he will follow Christ. Paul cannot accept the

111

punishment of anyone else's sins. Only Christ can take our place. Nobody but you can make the decision for your salvation.

If you are a Christian, read Paul's words again. How much do you care whether anyone comes to know Christ? These people for whom Paul grieved were not even known to him personally. He just didn't want his fellow countrymen to be lost without Christ. Can you join with Paul in his concern? Do you want to?

Make a prayer list of those you would like to see come to know the Lord Jesus Christ. Pray for them. Ask the Lord if there is something you can do to give them a desire to know Christ. Be an example of what a Christian should be.

5th Day   Heirs of the Promise   Romans 9:6-13

It is so easy to become overcome with our own shortcomings or failures. We live in such a complicated world that it seems impossible to succeed all the time. Perhaps now and then we may feel that it is almost impossible to succeed at all. So many times our problem seems to be that we know what we should do but somehow we just can't seem to do it.

The Lord knows us and He knows our shortcomings and He assures us that His "blessings are not given just because someone decides to have them or works hard to get them. They are given because God takes pity on those He wants to" (verse 16, *LNT*).

Our responsibility is to receive Jesus Christ as our Saviour; to take by faith God's gift of forgiveness and new life in Christ. Then, we rest in God, confident that He will do for us all that He has promised.

Jacob was far from perfect, but God forgave him for his sins and Jacob went on. Our sins are fact. There is no denying that we have failed miserably. But Christ has forgiven us. Now, we are to go on—striving to please Him and to obey Him, but assured that when we receive Him we become the heirs of the promises of God.

Paul told these truths to the Romans. He said, "This means that not all of Abraham's children are children of God, but only those who believe the promise of salvation which He made to Abraham" (verse 8, *LNT*). Then Paul closed the chapter with this assurance: "Those who believe in Him [Jesus] will never be disappointed" (verse 33, *LNT*).

Get your eyes off of your failures and shortcomings and onto the Lord Jesus Christ. In Him you will never be disappointed!

For further consideration, read all of Romans 9. Look for the things which Paul says God does for His children. Notice the problems that the Jews had because they could not rest in God's promises and obey Him. What can you learn from these lists that apply to your own life?

6th Day   Now Is the Time!
Romans 13:11-14

You pick up the morning paper and you read of a war here and increased tension there, a riot in this place and violence in that place. Do you feel that the future is nothing but darkness and gloom?

Then, read again the passage for today. Do you see the brightness ahead? Christ is coming again! His coming is nearer now than when you first met Him.

When times looked darkest for Jacob, God did not forget. His brother was angry because Jacob had stolen his blessing. Jacob had to leave home. Alone in a dark and strange place, God met him right there. There is no time so bleak but that a Christian cannot look up assured that God is with him.

Do you look with anticipation for the Lord's return? Early Christians greeted each other with the assuring word, "The Lord is coming!" Does that thought enter your mind? In days of frustration it is good to know that the future rests in the Lord's hands and that someday He will come and make everything right.

As we await His coming, we are nevertheless to be concerned with our lives now and the work of making Christ known. That's what Paul was telling the Romans in the passage which we read and that is what he says to us. We might paraphrase his words like this: "Look for the Lord's return, anticipate it with eagerness, but still remember that there are people who need to meet Christ, and your life is an influence toward their decision."

The last verse of this chapter is the summary. Mr. Phillips translates it like this: "Let us be Christ's men from head to foot, and give no chances to the flesh to have its fling."

Are you Christ's man from head to foot?

For further consideration, read II Peter 3. These are verses in which Peter describes the coming of Christ. In them you will note a question in verse 11, "What manner of persons ought ye to be?" How do you answer that question in the light of the Scriptures you have read?

7th Day   There's Always the Other Fellow
Romans 14:1–4

The accounts of Jacob and Esau which form the basis for this week's study are examples of a disregard for the truths set forth in Romans. Neither of these boys thought about the other. Each was concerned only with himself.

The problem before us is that we too find it all too easy to disregard the other fellow. We sit and condemn the Esaus because they are too earthly minded. Then we turn right around and condemn the Jacobs because we do not agree with their methods. We all too often have our little list of what we consider to be correct responses to specific situations and measure everyone by our little list.

Now the Bible says that we must not indulge in this pastime. God receives people and forgives people; He does not receive behavior and forgive behavior. That's what Paul said in verse 3: "God hath received him." We condemn the behavior and never see the man behind the problem. If we use Christ's analogy, we are so busy trying to pick the speck out of the other fellow's eye that we do not see that our self-righteousness may well be a two-by-four in our own eyes.

Read verse 4 again. Then listen to it in two other translations. First, *Living New Testament:* "They are God's servants, not yours. They are responsible to Him, not to you. Let Him tell them whether they are right or wrong. And God is able to make them do as they should." Now from *The New Testament in Modern English:* "After all, who are you to criticize the servant of somebody else, especially when that somebody else is God? It is to his own master that he gives, or fails to give, satisfactory service. And don't doubt that satisfaction, for God is well able to transform men into servants who are satisfactory."

That means He can even transform you and me!

For further consideration, read all of Romans 14 and the first three verses of Romans 15. What can you find in these verses which will guide you in your conduct and handling of a new Christian?

The setting for the Scriptures which we have read is the advantage that Jacob took over Esau and Jacob's getting Esau's birthright. All week we have read from various parts of the Bible guidelines for our actions and thoughts. We have read of the need for peace with others. We have read of the law of love which should motivate our lives. We have read of the coming of Christ and of our need to live obediently in anticipation. We have read that we should be patient and should not condemn someone who does not agree with our behavioral code. In other words, we have been reading about us and other Christians.

In a series like this dealing with relationships, we are wise to take the readings personally. First of all, consider your relationship with Christ. Do you really know Him as your Lord and Saviour?

Now, what of you and other Christians? Is there some work that you need to do to get the Lord to file away some rough places?

Now, you and the people who do not know your Lord—what do you need to do in their behalf?

Spend some time with the Lord and consider all these questions. Then, formulate your plans for action. Do what you have planned—looking to the Lord for strength day by day.

Chapter 12

THE LONG ROAD BACK

What can God do with someone who comes to Him? This story of Jacob is one answer to the question. It is interesting to note that the first time Jacob met the Lord at Bethel he was ready to get what he wanted by bargaining. Jacob had gone a long way down. The stealing of Esau's blessing hardly qualifies Jacob for the good conduct medal. Even his bargaining with God doesn't make one swell with pride in his behalf.

But don't give up on Jacob. Remember God didn't give up. Jacob had a long road to walk. He had a number of experiences before him. But he walked the road and he endured the experiences and God met him and transformed Jacob into Israel, promising him the fulfillment of the covenant.

Bible reading for this week: Genesis 27:18-24; 28:11-17; 46:1-5.

1st Day   Not by Myself   II Corinthians 3:1-6

Jacob had every reason to feel he was a failure as he made his way north from Beersheba. He must have been traveling three days when he came to Bethel. Here he wrapped himself in his cloak, lay on the ground, a stone for a pillow, and went to sleep. Jacob had failed all the way around. God had told his mother that he was to be the leader of the family, and here he was running away—some leader!

Then, everything changed, because God appeared to Jacob and told him that he was not alone. This was the beginning of the way back. It did not mean that Jacob never stumbled again. He did. But it did mean that now he knew he walked with God.

You and I may be a lot like Jacob. We, too, often feel that we are running from failure. Or at least from frustration. Alone, we fail. But we don't have to go alone.

Paul told the people of Corinth that he trusted what God had done in their lives. His trust was not in them but in Christ and He never failed.

When we know Christ, this is our story too. Alone, we are doomed. But with Christ, trusting in His strength, it is a different story. "We dare to say such things because of the confidence we have in God through Christ. Not that we are in any way confident of our own resources. It is he [God] who makes us competent administrators" (verses 4-6, Phillips).

Because of Christ, you can say the same words. Your abilities are dependent on His strength!

For further consideration, read Philippians 4. This is Paul's autobiography regarding the strength and peace which he finds in Christ. Look for the things that Paul says the Lord does and gives to him. Look for what Paul does in the power of Christ. Do you really believe these things are true for you?

2nd Day   Constant or Fading?
II Corinthians 3:12–18

Did you notice that in the passage two examples of "glory" are given? The first speaks of the glory of God in connection with Moses and we might add our reading concerning Jacob. Jacob came to Bethel and saw the vision of God at the top of a ladder. He heard God's promise that He would be with Jacob (Genesis 28:16). But Jacob left Bethel and journeyed into the problems in the house of Laban. He had to come back to Bethel for renewal of his commitment to God. He had to wrestle with the angel of the Lord at Jabbok. For Jacob, Bethel was an experience.

In II Corinthians Paul speaks of Moses, the man of God who spoke with the Lord and came back to the camp of Israel with his face glowing with the radiance of the Lord. He covered his face because the people of Israel were afraid to look at him. Paul says he covered it too, because the glory was fading and he did not want the people to realize this.

Then comes the contrast. In verse 18 Paul says: "But all of us who are Christians have no veils on our faces, but reflect like mirrors the glory of the Lord. We are transfigured in ever-increasing splendor into his own image" (Phillips). What a privilege we have. We do not have experiences with the Lord; we live in the presence of Christ. We are like mirrors; we reflect the image of the one in whose presence we are. Did you notice that instead of God's glory fading, Paul says we go on "from glory to glory." Our life with Christ gets better and better and we grow and mature into the person God would have us to be, as we become more and more like Christ.

For further consideration, read Ephesians 4:11–32. Here Paul goes into detail concerning what he means by growing and maturing in Christ. What does He say happens to the Christian as he matures? What are you to do as a result of this maturity? Notice especially the practical instructions regarding your daily walk and habits.

3rd Day   Better and Better
II Corinthians 5:1–5

After Jacob's vision at Bethel, he awoke and we read, "And he was afraid, and said, How dreadful is this place! this is none other but the house of God, and this is the gate of heaven" (Genesis 28:17).

It can be a terrifying thought to contemplate being in the presence of God. That is, terrifying if we do not really know Him. Paul must have had this in mind and, wanting to reassure us, he wrote the words we read today in our Scripture.

We will have to remember that the comfort which Paul outlines in this Scripture applies only to those who know Jesus Christ as their own Saviour. For the others—Jacob's feeling may be multiplied. The writer of Hebrews says: "It is a fearful thing to fall into the hands of the living God" (Hebrews 10:31). And he is right!

But for a Christian, the future holds no such terrors.

"For we know that when this tent we live in now is taken down—when we die and leave these bodies—we will have wonderful new bodies in heaven, homes that will be ours forevermore, made for us by God Himself, and not by human hands" (verse 1, *LNT*).

Instead of the future being a terror for the Christian, it is an expectation. "Our homeland is in heaven, with our Saviour the Lord Jesus Christ and we are looking forward to His return from there. When He comes back He will take these dying bodies of ours and change them into glorious bodies like His own, using the same mighty power that He will use to conquer all else everywhere" (Philippians 3:20,21, *LNT*).

For further consideration, read Revelation 21:22—22:7. Read and meditate upon these descriptions of what awaits a Christian. Doesn't the realization of these things make you want to serve the Lord better and show your gratitude to Him more constantly? How will you accomplish your desires?

4th Day   Just Passing Through
II Corinthians 5:6-10

These verses in II Corinthians are really a continuation of what we read yesterday. Paul is going on with the same thoughts regarding the future of the Christian. Before we consider what he has to say, think for a few minutes of Jacob.

The second time that Jacob met the Lord was on his way back from Laban. Twenty years had passed since the vision of the ladder at Bethel. Now, Jacob was about to meet Esau again. He wasn't sure how pleasant that meeting would be. In preparation Jacob stayed alone on one side of the Brook Jabbok. There he wrestled with the angel of the Lord and pleaded for a blessing. He received his blessing and then we read: "And Jacob called the name of the place Peniel: for I have seen God face to face, and my life is preserved. And as he passed over Penuel the sun rose upon him" (Genesis 32:30,31).

The day came just as any other day and Jacob went out to meet it and Esau. The experience of the night was over and he had a new day to face.

We have read today of the coming of the Lord, we have read of the promises of the future for the Christian. But there is today to live—while we look forward to the time when we shall be with the Lord. Paul says he is willing to be what God wants him to be—one day at a time. If he is here, he is absent from the Lord. If God takes him, he will be present with the Lord.

The same is true for us. We know that the future holds great things for us—the Bible says so and we believe it. But, for today, we are here. The sun rose upon us this morning and we are expected to meet the problems and challenges of today while we are passing through to our eternal home in heaven.

How do we live today? Look at verse 7 in II Corinthians 5. "For we walk by faith, not by sight." We received the Lord Jesus by faith. We walk by faith. We know the Lord. We are confident that we can depend on Him. We walk trusting Him.

Jacob went on to meet Esau. We go about our duties whatever they are. We have met the Lord, face to face. We trust Him. Now, we go about the job of living day-by-day, one day at a time.

We know Christ cannot help but make a difference

in our lives. But really, what difference does He make in a day-by-day experience?

What does it mean to you to walk by faith, not sight? How do you know you are walking by faith?

5th Day   What Constrains?
II Corinthians 5:11–15

What constrains us? That's a good question. The word Paul uses in verse 14 is translated in several ways: controls, impels, presses in on all sides, urges, rules, compels, is the very spring of our actions. We might say, "What is the driving force of our actions?"

With Jacob it was an intense desire for the birthright. He bought it from Esau; he stole the blessing from his brother; he even tried through Rachel to get the symbol of Laban's birthright, the household gods. He bargained with God that the Lord let him return to his father's house. He even wrestled all night to be sure to get a blessing. There is no doubt about it—the birthright and all that it signified was the constraining force in Jacob.

What about us? What constrains us? It might be security for the future, a good name among friends and business associates, success by our own definition of the word. Any number of things might be the driving force in our lives.

Paul said that the force which impelled him was the love of Christ. Paul took a look at Christ. He realized that He is the Son of God. He knew that Christ became a man and was identified with us. He thought of how Christ died and why He died. He thought of the hopelessness of trying to attain to forgiveness without the intervention of Christ. He realized that through the death of Christ, he had forgiveness and eternal life. He thought of all these things and Paul said the love of Christ controlled his life. It was as though he said, "I cannot do anything without realizing what Christ has done for me. Knowing this, I cannot help but love and serve him." To Paul it seemed obvious that all he could do now was to live for Christ.

We are back to where we started. What constrains you?

For further consideration, read Psalm 27. David is desiring to know God better. The psalm is a prayer and a list of imperatives. Read it carefully. Make your own list of what you want to do with regard to your relationship to the Lord. Pray your own prayer.

6th Day   What Happened to You?
II Corinthians 5:16–21

Jacob made an uneasy peace with Laban (Genesis 31:51, 52). He was reconciled to Esau (33:4). He apparently patched up things with his father Isaac (35:27). Most important of all, he was forgiven by God (35:11–13). All of these things are true, yet Jacob had to settle for much less than God gives you in Christ.

Paul told the Corinthians in verse 17 that those who believe in Christ and receive Him as their Saviour are new creatures. You have a new nature. Mr. Phillips says it like this in his translation: "For if a man is in Christ he becomes a new person altogether—the past is finished and gone, everything has become fresh and new."

As a new person you have been reconciled to God by Jesus Christ. Listen again to Mr. Phillips in verse 18: "All this is God's doing, for he has reconciled us to himself through Jesus Christ." It is all God's doing. He gives us more than we can ever imagine is possible.

Because we are new creatures and have been reconciled with God, it is possible for us to assume a new responsibility. We can be ambassadors for Christ—His official representatives, agents in an alien world, representing the Lord before men, speaking in His behalf. "He has made us agents of the reconciliation. God was in Christ personally reconciling the world to himself—not counting their sins against them—and has commissioned us with the message of reconciliation. We are now Christ's ambassadors, as though God were appealing direct to you through us. As his personal representative we say, 'Make your peace with God'" (verses 18–20, Phillips).

Not only may you have the joy and peace of knowing that everything is right between you and God, but you may also be His personal representative in the world to bring others to know the same joy and peace you have!

For further consideration, look up the word "ambassador" in the dictionary. How may you appropriate the definition to your commission from God? Do the same with the word "reconcile."

7th Day   Christ the Mediator   John 1:43–51

We have thought several times this week of Jacob's experience at Bethel (Genesis 28). We certainly agree that the experience was a terrifying and yet a satisfying one for Jacob. The ladder reaching to heaven, angels going up and down on it, the Lord speaking to Jacob from above it. All this was something Jacob certainly never forgot.

Now we turn today to the New Testament and the Lord speaking to Nathanael. "And he saith unto him, Verily, verily, I say unto you, Hereafter ye shall see heaven open, and the angels of God ascending and descending upon the Son of man" (verse 51). The "ladder" between earth and heaven is none other than the Lord Jesus Christ Himself.

When Paul explained this truth to Timothy he said, "For there is one God, and there is one who brings God and men together, the man Christ Jesus, who gave himself to redeem all men" (I Timothy 2:5, *TEV*).

Christ is our access to God for salvation. He is the entrance in prayer. "If ye shall ask anything in my name, I will do it" (John 14:14). Christ is the means by whom we may have fellowship with God. "God is faithful, by whom ye were called unto the fellowship of his Son Jesus Christ our Lord" (I Corinthians 1:9). All that we need is in Christ and Christ is all that we need. "For living to me means simply 'Christ,' and if I die I should merely gain more of him" (Philippians 1:21, Phillips).

What can you add to the list that tells what Christ is to you? Use a concordance or Bible dictionary to help. Think of the gifts He gives, the needs He supplies for your daily round of activities.

We started this week thinking of the question, "What can God do with someone who comes to Him?" All week we have been reading the answer from various parts of the Bible. Now, we are ready to think through the answer. He can supply the strength to make our abilities count for Him. We can be mirrors that reflect the glory of Christ and woo people to Him as the Holy Spirit works in our lives. We can look forward to the time when we shall have glorious bodies like Christ's. We can walk by faith, confident of Christ who leads us. We can be constrained by the love of Christ. We can be reconciled to God and join in the ministry of reconciliation as His ambassadors. We can find that life really is Christ, and enjoy every minute that He gives us.

All this God can do for someone who comes to Him. Do you really want Him to do it for you?

Chapter 13

YET TO COME

Grudges are many times the cause of the greatest heartbreak. Refusal to forgive, halfhearted forgiveness ("I'll forgive, but I'll never forget"), forgiveness that constantly keeps the other person in your debt, all of these make for friction which is bound to flare up into disastrous personal relationships.

Today we turn to Joseph, the man who learned what forgiveness really meant. He becomes one of the great examples in the Old Testament of the ability to recognize the hand of God in adversity.

Since we want to know forgiveness at its best, we shall also turn to the New Testament and read of the example of our Lord.

Bible reading for this week: Genesis 44:18-34.

1st Day   He Knows You
John 10:1-6

The story of Joseph is the story of wrongdoing and forgiveness. We read in the introductory Scripture the account of his proving his brothers' worthiness. Joseph wanted to be sure that they had changed their attitude toward their father's favorite son, Benjamin. They passed the test and Joseph forgave them.

When we turn to the Scripture for today we find the Lord Jesus speaking of His relationship with His sheep: people like us who do not deserve anything but judgment from His hand. We cannot pass any test of worthiness. But our failure does not affect the Lord's care for us. In spite of what we are God loves and forgives us.

Notice what the Lord says about "His sheep." They hear His voice and they come (verse 3). That is what makes them His sheep. Sheep recognize their shepherd and come to Him. When you and I recognize that we need the Lord and the forgiveness He offers, we come to Him by grace; through faith we receive Him and become His sheep.

He knows us. Christians are never crowds to the Lord. He knows us individually. He knows the things that trouble us. He knows the things that thrill us. He knows our good times and our not so good. He knows us by name.

He leads and we follow. What a thoughtful arrangement. We never go anywhere without the Lord there before us. He approves the way and the destination. All we need to do is follow along behind Him.

How do you follow? You know His voice. You know it because you read His word, because you talk things over with Him in prayer, because you seek in every way you know to be the kind of "sheep" He wants. The more you do these things the better you know His voice and the easier it is to follow His leading.

For further consideration, read all of John 10. The Lord has much more to say about you, His sheep, and Himself, your Shepherd. Look for the characteristics of each. What difference does this reading make in the way you will "follow" today?

2nd Day   The Good Shepherd
John 10:7–18

Yesterday we read that the Lord Jesus, our shepherd, cares for us. Today we read the section which tells us how much He cares.

Verse 11: The Good Shepherd gives His life for His sheep. The key word is "gives." The death of Christ is voluntary. He made that clear in verse 18; no one takes His life from Him. The Lord was never caught in a stream of evil he could not escape. He gave Himself that His sheep might live.

Verse 12 tells us by implication that the shepherd does not leave his sheep. The Good Shepherd is always close-by. You cannot escape Him. But neither can you be scattered beyond His watchful eye.

Verse 14 is a reminder of what we have already discovered: He knows His sheep and they know Him. Never a package deal on either side. It is a personal commitment on the part of each individual that makes him one of the Lord's sheep. And then He is personally known by the Good Shepherd!

Verse 16 is another important implication. The flock

is not yet complete. There are still other sheep who must become His sheep. When these sheep really hear the voice of the Shepherd they will follow Him.

There is the Great Commission given in the picture of sheep and shepherd. Our duty is to tell them of the Shepherd we know and love and follow. Then He brings them to Himself.

If the bringing of other sheep depends on us, how likely is it they will hear?

What is your church doing about the "other sheep"? Some of them may be on the other side of the world. Some may be living next door to you. Update your prayer list for those who seek to make Christ known. Ask the Lord what part you should have.

3rd Day   More than Forgiven   John 15:1-11

We cannot belittle the act of Joseph in forgiving his brothers. It was hard and we can be sure it was genuine. But the brothers could never bring themselves to accept the fact that they were really forgiven. They worried about what would happen when their father died. Read Genesis 50:15-21.

Do you ever wonder how God could so completely forgive you? Read again the verses from John 15. You see the Lord did so much more for us than Joseph could ever do for his brothers. The Lord said that those who have been born again are united with Him as closely as a branch is attached to a vine. The same life that is in the vine is in the branch. The life which the Lord gives to us is His life, eternal life.

Verse 5 says that we are not just cleansed but that we are so closely united to Christ that our strength and our capabilities come through Him. We cannot work alone to do His will, but He says we do not have to try.

Verse 7 says that we are not just strengthened but that we may ask Him for the things that we want and He will give them as they are best for us and bring glory to His name.

Verse 8 says that we are not just given the fellowship of prayer but that we may bring forth the fruit of the Spirit in our lives. It will be the life of Christ bearing fruit to His glory. See Galatians 5:22, 23.

Verse 9 says that we are not just fruit-bearing branches, but that we are loved by Christ. In fact, He says that He loves us as God loves Him. And according to verse 10 we may continue in His love by simple obedience to His commands.

Verse 11 is almost obvious when we consider all that the Lord has said. How can our joy be anything but full?

Do you ever stop and just praise and thank the Lord for all that you have in Christ? This would be a good day to emphasize thanksgiving. If you have real needs, ask Him to fill them, but concentrate on thanking the Lord for what He has already done.

4th Day   Not Servants but Friends
John 15:12-17

When Joseph's brothers came to him after Jacob's death they were willing to do anything to save themselves. "And his brethren also went and fell down before his face; and they said, behold, we be thy servants" (Genesis 50:18). The very point that started the whole trouble was now readily acceptable in their sight. If living meant being Joseph's servants they were willing to pay the price.

Do you feel that way when you think about your relationship to God? After all, if the only way to survive includes slavery to the Lord, you would be willing to be a slave. The apostle Paul agreed with that feeling. On a number of occasions he called himself a bondslave of Christ. Just to get a toehold on heaven is all any of us should expect. Is that the way you feel?

Then, read the Lord's words to His disciples again. " 'There is no greater love than this—that a man should lay down his life for his friends. You are my friends if you do what I tell you to do. I shall not call you servants any longer, for a servant does not share his master's confidence. No, I call you friends, now, because I have told you everything that I have heard from the Father.' "

" 'It is not that you have chosen me; but it is I who have chosen you' " (John 15:13-16, Phillips).

Perhaps you would be satisfied with being a servant, but apparently the Lord is not satisfied with that status for you. You are His friend if you have come to Him for salvation. He died for His friends—He died for you. He confides in His friends—He confides in you through His Word and through the Holy Spirit within you. He chooses His friends—He chose you. He gives a responsibility to His friends—He gives one to you: obey Him and let the Spirit of God bear the fruit of the Spirit in your life. He gives His friends a special privilege—He gives one to you: "Whatsoever ye shall ask of the Father in my name, he may give it you." Now, he says to His friends: "Love one another."

What do you want in a friend? What makes a person a friend? Does Christ fulfill your requirements toward you? Do you fulfill them toward Him?

5th Day   It Won't Be Easy!   John 15:18-27

To be accepted by people who matter is one of the great desires of all of us. We like to be liked. All week we have been reading how we may be accepted by God. We have read of the Good Shepherd and of all that He does for us when we are His sheep. We have read of the close association that is possible between us and our Lord when He likened us to the branches and Himself to the vine. We have read that we are His friends, and that He has chosen us for this position. The accent has been consistently on the wonderful truth that we have been accepted by God for Christ's sake and that He has done so much for us, His children.

Now, today we read an entirely different story. The Lord showed His disciples that living for Him was realistic. The Christian life is not a hothouse existence where the temperature is always to our liking and the humidity is controlled for our comfort. Christians live in the real world of conflicts and misunderstandings. Remember the point that we have learned—the conflicts are not between the Christian and the Lord. He has graciously forgiven, cleansed and received us. The conflict comes because there are those in the world who do not know Him.

In every other relationship in this world, the case holds true: take a firm stand on one side of an issue and immediately you will meet opposition. It is true in politics, in business, in family relationships, everywhere. How can we ever dream that we can take a firm stand for Christ and not find opposition? This is what the Lord is talking about in the verses which we read today.

Take a firm stand for Christ and the world will be against you. Take a stand with the world, and face God's displeasure. When you think about it that way, your option is hardly worthy of consideration.

For further consideration, read Luke 9:57–61 and 14:25–35. The Lord is talking about discipleship. What do you think He is saying about the cost of being a disciple? What has it cost you? Is the price really too high for you?

6th Day   Is It Really Best for Me?
John 16:1–11

From the viewpoint of a full life lived in service to the people of Egypt and even to his own family, Joseph looked back and assured his brothers, "As for you, ye thought evil against me; but God meant it unto good, to bring to pass, as it is this day" (Genesis 50:20). Do you suppose he could have realized this fact when he was a part of the Ishmaelite caravan headed for slavery in Egypt? Or, during the temptations in the house of Potiphar? Or, when the butler forgot his promise and Joseph waited in prison two years?

Consider the disciples of the Lord on the last night before the Lord's death. Do you think they found it a simple thing to agree with the Lord when He said, "The fact of the matter is that it is best for you that

I go away" (John 16:7, *LNT*)? Remember He had just told them that they could do nothing without Him. Now, He says He is leaving them and that it is good for them that He does.

How is your confidence in the Lord? Do you have to understand what He does in your life at the time He does it? Christ said, "What man is there of you, whom if his son ask bread, will he give him a stone? . . . If ye then, being evil, know how to give good gifts unto your children, how much more shall your Father which is in heaven give good things to them that ask him?" (Matthew 7:9,11).

Can you accept what comes from God's hand confident that it is bread, even if it feels as hard as a stone? Do you really believe that what He gives you is best for you?

For further consideration, read James 1. Notice what he says about trials and testings. Do you agree with him? Read the chapter in at least one of the newer translations also.

7th Day   Tomorrow!   John 16:16-24

Joseph took care of his brothers, as he promised, as long as he lived. But when we turn to the first chapter of Exodus we read, "Now there arose a new king over Egypt, which knew not Joseph" (verse 8). The influence and power of Joseph was ended and the Israelites became slaves of the Egyptians.

How different when we turn to the New Testament passage. The Lord told His disciples that He was to die, that He was to leave them. But He is God and the story does not end in death. We thought yesterday of the hard times which sometimes come into our lives. But this is not the end for us either.

Listen to the words of Christ: "Now you are going through pain, but I shall see you again and your hearts will thrill with joy—the joy that no one can take away from you—and on that day you will not ask me any questions" (verses 22, 23, Phillips). The day is coming when you will be satisfied—no questions, no wonderings, everything made plain.

The future is all bound up in the knowledge that the Lord Jesus will come again. Paul writing to Titus called this the "blessed hope" of the Christian. The knowledge that the Lord will come and we will be with Him forever is sufficient to get us through whatever today may bring. We can agree with the psalmist, "Weeping may endure for a night, but joy cometh in the morning" (Psalm 30:5).

"For the free gift of eternal salvation is now being offered to everyone; And along with this gift comes the realization that God wants us to turn from godless living and sinful pleasures and to live good, God-fearing lives day after day, Looking forward to that time when His glory shall be seen—the glory of our great God and Saviour Jesus Christ, Who died under God's judgment against our sins, so that He could rescue us from constant falling into sin and make us His very own people, with cleansed hearts and real enthusiasm for doing kind things for others" (Titus 2:11–14, LNT).

When the Lord finished speaking the words we have been reading He prayed for the disciples and for us. For further consideration, read His prayer in John 17. Notice what the Lord asked for concerning you and your relationship with Him.

We have come to the end of the study of Genesis

and the Christian life. We have read much Scripture and considered a number of individuals. We have looked especially at our Lord and Saviour Jesus Christ. We have seen what He has done for us and what He plans for our future.

Now think back over what you have read. Look at some of the notes you have made. What difference will your reading and study make in your daily life?

Perhaps this is a time of rededication for you. Perhaps you are meeting Christ for the first time. Whatever your position may be, talk to the Lord about it. Then, go out in the strength He provides and with the power of the Holy Spirit within you to be what the Lord has shown you you should be.